2nd Workshop on EVENTS: Definition, Detection, Coreference, and Representation 2014

Held at ACL 2014

Baltimore, Maryland, USA
22 – 27 June 2014

ISBN: 978-1-63439-209-9

Printed from e-media with permission by:

Curran Associates, Inc.
57 Morehouse Lane
Red Hook, NY 12571

proceedings.com

Some format issues inherent in the e-media version may also appear in this print version.

Printed by Curran Associates, Inc. (2014)

For permission requests, please contact the Association for Computational Linguistics at the address below.

Association for Computational Linguistics
209 N. Eighth Street
Stroudsburg, Pennsylvania 18360

Phone: 1-570-476-8006
Fax: 1-570-476-0860

acl@aclweb.org

Additional copies of this publication are available from:

Curran Associates, Inc.
57 Morehouse Lane
Red Hook, NY 12571 USA
Phone: 845-758-0400
Fax: 845-758-2634
Email: curran@proceedings.com
Web: www.proceedings.com

Introduction

Although events have long been a subject of study, the NLP community has yet to achieve a consensus on the treatment of events, in spite of their critical importance to several areas in natural language processing, such as topic detection and tracking, information extraction, question answering, textual entailment, causality, and anomaly and contradiction detection. This, the second, EVENTS workshop brings together people for a discussion about the nature, definition, recognition, and representation of events. In this workshop we will structure the discussion around three themes.

- Event Ontology: A comparison of ontology resources
- Event Structure: Subevent coreference and script learning
- Event Mentions: Recognizing mentions of events in text

During the discussion, we will cover the following topics, among others:

- Event Coreference Detection (Full and/or Partial)
- Event Mention Detection
- Event Extraction
- Event Ontology
- Event Scripts
- Evaluations of Event Detection
- Issues in Event Annotation

An important aspect will be preparations for a pilot evaluation on event mention detection to be held at the end of 2014. Jerry Hobbs, ISI/USC, will be the keynote speaker, with an address entitled "Implicit Causal Relations among Events in Text". We will have 10 poster presentations during the workshop. We hope that this second Events workshop will support the continuing efforts of the research community in coming to grips with this challenging topic.

Organizers:
Teruko Mitamura, CMU
Eduard Hovy, CMU
Martha Palmer, University of Colorado

Organizers:

Teruko Mitamura, Carnegie Mellon University
Eduard Hovy, Carnegie Mellon University
Martha Palmer, University of Colorado Boulder

Program Committee:

Rodolfo Delmonte (Università Ca' Foscari, Venice – Italy)
Marjorie Freedman (BBN)
Robert Frederking (Carnegie Mellon University)
Kira Griffit (LDC)
Heng Ji (CUNY)
Boyan Onyshkevych (DOD)
James Pustejovsky (Brandeis University)
Marta Recasens (Google Inc.)
Ian Soboroff, (NIST)
Stephanie Strassel (LDC)
Mihai Surdeanu (University of Arizona)
Lucy Vanderwende (Microsoft)
Benjamin van Durme (Johns Hopkins University)
Piek Vossen (VU University Amsterdam)
Luke Zettlemoyer (University of Washington)

Invited Speaker:

Jerry Hobbs (ISI/USC)

Table of Contents

Conference Program

Friday, June 27, 2014

9:00-9:15 Welcome

9:15-10:30 **Invited Talk: Implicit Causal Relations among Events in Text**
Speaker: Jerry Hobbs, ISI/USC

10:30-11:00 Break

11:00-12:00 **Session I: The Nature of Events**
Chair: Teruko Mitamura, Carnegie Mellon University

12:00-1:00 Lunch Break

1:00-2:30 **Poster Session**

Augmenting FrameNet Via PPDB
Pushpendre Rastogi and Benjamin Van Durme

Verbal Valency Frame Detection and Selection in Czech and English
Ondřej Dušek, Jan Hajic and Zdenka Uresova

Challenges of Adding Causation to Richer Event Descriptions
Rei Ikuta, Will Styler, Mariah Hamang, Tim O'Gorman and Martha Palmer

Inter-annotator Agreement for ERE annotation
Seth Kulick, Ann Bies and Justin Mott

Unsupervised Techniques for Extracting and Clustering Complex Events in News
Delia Rusu, James Hodson and Anthony Kimball

Conceptual and Practical Steps in Event Coreference Analysis of Large-scale Data
Fatemeh Torabi Asr, Jonathan Sonntag, Yulia Grishina and Manfred Stede

A Comparison of the Events and Relations Across ACE, ERE, TAC-KBP, and FrameNet Annotation Standards
Jacqueline Aguilar, Charley Beller, Paul McNamee, Benjamin Van Durme, Stephanie Strassel, Zhiyi Song and Joe Ellis

Is the Stanford Dependency Representation Semantic?
Rachel Rudinger and Benjamin Van Durme

Friday, June 27, 2014 (continued)

	Qualities of Eventiveness Sean Monahan and Mary Brunson
	Evaluation for Partial Event Coreference Jun Araki, Eduard Hovy and Teruko Mitamura
2:30-3:30	**Session II: Event Ontology** Chair: Martha Palmer, University of Colorado Boulder
3:30-4:00	Break
4:00-5:00	**Session III: Event Structure and Subevents** Chair: Eduard Hovy, Carnegie Mellon University
5:00-6:00	**Session IV: Shared Task Presentations and Discussions**
6:00	Close

Augmenting FrameNet Via PPDB

Pushpendre Rastogi[1] and **Benjamin Van Durme**[1,2]
[1]Center for Language and Speech Processing
[2]Human Language Technology Center of Excellence
Johns Hopkins University
pushpendre@jhu.edu, vandurme@cs.jhu.edu

Abstract

FrameNet is a lexico-semantic dataset that embodies the theory of frame semantics. Like other semantic databases, FrameNet is incomplete. We augment it via the paraphrase database, PPDB, and gain a three-fold increase in coverage at 65% precision.

1 Introduction

Frame semantics describes the meaning of a word in relation to real world events and entities. In frame semantics the primary unit of lexical analysis is the *frame* and the *lexical unit*. A frame aims to capture the most salient properties of a concept, situation or event. For example, the frame representing the concept of `Abandonment` contains eight attributes:[1] `Agent`, `Theme`, `Place`, `Time`, `Manner`, `Duration`, `Explanation` and `Depictive`. A *lexical unit* is a tuple of three elements: the lemma of a word, its POS tag and the associated frame.

FrameNet is large lexico-semantic dataset that contains manually annotated information including frame descriptions, frame-frame relations and frame annotated sentences. It has been used build to frame semantic parsers, which are systems that can analyze a sentence and annotate its words with the frames that they evoke and the corresponding frame elements. The task of frame semantic parsing was introduced by Gildea and Jurafsky (2002) and later it matured into a community-wide shared task (Baker et al., 2007), with CMU's SEMAFOR system being the current state-of-the-art parser (Das et al., 2013).

Common to rich, manually constructed semantic resources, the coverage of FrameNet across its targetted language (English) is incomplete. State-of-the-art frame semantic parsers thus employ various heuristics to identify the frame evoked by out-of-vocabulary items (OOVs) at test-time.[2] For instance, an OOV if present in WordNet might be aligned to frame(s) assigned to in-vocabulary items in shared synsets (see the work by Ferrández et al. (2010) and the related works section therein). In this work we take a different approach and attempt to directly increase the coverage of the FrameNet corpus by automatically expanding the collection of training examples via PPDB, The Paraphrase Database (Ganitkevitch et al., 2013).

In Section 2 we analyze FrameNet and comment on the sparsity in its different parts. In Section 3 we describe PPDB, and how it was used to augment FrameNet. We present our evaluation experiments and results in the latter half of the section followed by conclusions.

2 FrameNet Coverage

FrameNet is a rich semantic resource, yet currently lacks complete coverage of the language. In the following we give examples of this incompleteness, in particular the OOV issue that we will focus on in latter sections.

Frames A frame represents an event, a situation or a real life concept; FrameNet version 1.5 contains 1,019 such frames. These thousand frames do not cover all possible situations that we might encounter. For example, FrameNet does not have a frame for the activity of `Programming` even though it has frames for `Creating`, `Text_Creation`, etc. The situa-

[1]An attribute of a frame is also called a *Frame Element*.

[2]For example the *Abandonment* frame lacks *jettison* as one of its lexical units, and further, that word is not listed as a lexical unit in FrameNet v1.5, making *jettison* an OOV.

Proceedings of the 2nd Workshop on EVENTS: Definition, Detection, Coreference, and Representation, pages 1–5,
Baltimore, Maryland, USA, June 22-27, 2014.

tion of writing a computer program is stereotypical and attributes that a reader might associate with such an activity are: agent (who wrote the program), language (the programming language used) and function (the program's purpose).

Further, FrameNet's granularity is at times uneven. For example, the Explosion frame and the Become_Triggered frames do not have agentive attributes, instead there exist separate frames Detonate_Explosive and Triggering which have the attributes Agent and Actor respectively. This suggests a pattern that events which are frequently described without an agent are assigned their own frames. However, there is no Burial frame which focuses on the event corresponding to frame of Burying, which itself focuses on the Actor.

This difference in granularity could be resolved by either making distinctions more evenly fine-grained: trying to automatically inducing new frames; or by making things more evenly-coarse grained: automatically merging existing frames that are deemed similar. Researchers have explored methods for automatically learning frames and on learning collocations of frames to their syntactic dependent phrases. Recent examples include using either a Bayesian topic model to learn clusters of words (O' Connor, 2012; Materna, 2012), or attempting to learn symbolic concepts and attributes from dictionary definitions of words (Orfan and Allen, 2013).

Frame-Frame Relations FrameNet encodes certain types of correlations between situations and events by adding defeasible typed-relations between frames encoding pairwise dependencies.

There are eight types of frame-frame relations: Inherits_from, Perspective_on, Precedes, Subframe_of, See_also, Uses, Is_Inchoative_of, and Is_Causative_of.[3] For example the frame Being_Born is related to Death through the relation Is_Preceded_By. Such commonsense knowledge of event-event relationships would be of significant utility to general AI, however it is a large space to fill: with 1,019 frames and 8 binary relations there is a large upper bound on the number of total possible relation pairs, even if not considering the previous issue of incomplete frame coverage. For example, the Experience_bodily_harm and Hostile_encounter frames are not related through the Is_Causative_Of relation, even though it is reasonable to expect that a hostile encounter would result in bodily harm.[4] Though researchers have used FrameNet relations for tasks such as recognizing textual entailment (RTE) (Aharon et al., 2010) and for text understanding (Fillmore and Baker, 2001), to the best of our knowledge there has been no work on automatically extending frame-frame relations.

Frame Annotated Sentences FrameNet contains annotated sentences providing examples of: lexical units, frames those lexical units evoked, and frame elements present in the sentence (along with additional information). These annotated sentences can be divided into two types based on whether all the frame evoking words were marked as targets or not.

The first type, which we call lexicographic, contains sentences with a single target per sentence. The second type, called fulltext, contains sentences that have been annotated more completely and they contain multiple targets per sentence. There are 4,026 fulltext sentences containing 23,921 targets. This data has proved to be useful for lexico-semantic tasks like RTE and paraphrasing e.g. (Aharon et al., 2010; Coyne and Rambow, 2009). As compared to PropBank (Palmer et al., 2005), which annotated all predicates occurring within a collection of pre-existing documents, FrameNet provides *examples*, but not a corpus that allows for directly estimating relative frequencies.

Frame-Lemma Mappings As said earlier, *lexical units* are tuples of the lemma form of a word, its POS-tag and its associated frame. One component of FrameNet is its information about which words/lemmas prompt a particular frame. An annotated word that evokes a frame in a sentence is referred to as a *Target*. There are two areas where these mappings could be incomplete: (1) lemmas contained within FrameNet may have alternate senses such that they should be placed in more Frames (or related: a currently missing frame might then give rise to another sense of

[3]Five frame-frame relations also have an antonym relation: Is_Used_by, Is_Inherited_by, Is_Perspectivized_in, Has_Subframe(s), Is_Preceded_by, however an antonym relation does not add any extra information over its corresponding relation.

[4]*Reasonable* highlights the issue that we would optimally like to know things that are even just possible/not-too-unlikely, even if not strictly entailed.

such a lemma); and (2) lemmas from the language may not be in FrameNet in any form. Most research on mitigating this limitation involves mapping FrameNet's frames to WordNet's synsets.[5] Fossati et al. (2013) explored the feasibility of crowdsourcing FrameNet coverage, using the distributed manual labor of Mechanical Turk to complete the lemma coverage.

3 Augmenting FrameNet with PPDB

In order to expand the coverage of FrameNet, we performed an initial study on the use of a new broad-coverage lexical-semantic resource, PPDB, to first add new lemmas as potential triggers for a frame, and then automatically rewrite existing example sentences with these new triggers. The eventual goal of would be to enable any existing FrameNet semantic parser to simply retrain on this expanded dataset, rather than needing to encode methods for dynamic OOV-resolution at test-time (such as employed by SEMAFOR).

PPDB Ganitkevitch et al. (2013) released a large collection of lexical, phrasal and syntactic paraphrases[6] collectively called PPDB. We used the lexical rules in PPDB to find potential paraphrases of target words of frame annotated sentences. A lexical rule in PPDB looks like the following:

```
[VB] ||| help ||| assist |||
p(e|f)=2.832, p(f|e)=1.551, ...
```

This rule conveys that the log-probability that *help* would be paraphrased by the word *assist* is -2.832 but the log probability of *assist* being paraphrased as *help* is -1.551.[7] Ganitkevitch et al. (2013) released quality-sorted subsets of the full (large) collection, varying in size from `S` to `XXXL` by applying thresholds over a linear combination of the feature values to prune away low quality paraphrases. They verified that the average human judgement score of randomly sampled paraphrases from smaller sized collections was higher than the average human judgement score of a random sample from a larger collection.

Approach We used the lexical rules sans features along with a 5-gram Kneser-Ney smoothed language model trained using KenLM (Heafield et al., 2013) on the raw English sequence of Annotated Gigaword (Napoles et al., 2012) to paraphrase the fulltext frame annotated sentences of FrameNet. We used a combination of the WordNet morphological analyzer and Morpha[8] for lemmatization and Morphg[9] for generation.

Evaluation We present our evaluation of the quantity and quality of generated paraphrases in this section. Note that we did not use syntactic reordering to generate the paraphrases. Also we paraphrased the frame evoking targets individually i.e. we did not consider combinations of paraphrases of individual targets to be a new paraphrase of a sentence and we ignored those frame evoking targets that contained multiple words.[10]

With the above mentioned constraints we conducted the following experiments with different sizes of PPDB. In Experiment 1 we generated a set of candidate paraphrases for every target word in a sentence by directly querying that word and its dictionary form in PPDB. In Experiment 2 we first enlarged the set of lexical units mapped to a frame by merging lexical units of frames that were related to the target word's frame through either of the following relations: `Is_Perspectivized_In`, `Is_Inherited_By`, `Has_Subframe (s)`. For example, if frame `A` has a subframe `B` then lexical units mapped to `A` can evoke `B`. We then queried PPDB to gather paraphrases for all the lexical units collected so far. This experiment simulates the situation where a frame has been mapped to a set of words, e.g. synsets in WordNet, so that every word in that larger set is a paraphrase of any word that evokes a frame. This procedure increases the average number of paraphrases mapped to a frame and we present those averages in Table 1.

For both these experiments we also calculated the incremental benefit of PPDB over WordNet by

[5] It is worth noting that substituting a larger automatically derived WordNet (as derived in Snow et al. (2004)) could improve the recall of some of the methods which automatically learn a mapping from FrameNet frames to WordNet synsets.

[6] *Lexical*: Two words with the same meaning; *phrasal*: two strings of words with the same meaning; *syntactic*: strings of surface words and non-terminal categories that have the same meaning. These strings are templates with the non-terminals serving the role of constraints over what can go in the blanks.

[7] See complete list at `http://github.com/jweese/thrax/wiki/Feature-functions`.

[8] `http://ilexir.co.uk/applications/rasp/download`

[9] `http://cl.naist.jp/~eric-n/ubuntu-nlp/pool/hardy/english/morph_0.0.20030918-2nlp1~0hardy1.tar.gz`

[10] Among fulltext sentences less than 3% of targets contained multiple tokens.

Database	Lexical Unit/Frame
Framenet	20.24
PPDB S	23.15
PPDB M	32.00
PPDB L	74.08
PPDB XL	214.99

Table 1: Average count of lexical units per frame for different sizes of PPDB in experiment 2.

The General Assembly should set aside **money** for a new state health lab , millions of doses of antiviral drugs and a fund to help meet basic needs after a disaster , a legislative panel recommended Thursday .
1: The General Assembly should set aside **cash** ...
2: The General Assembly should set aside **fund** ...
1: The General Assembly should set aside **dough** ...
3: The General Assembly should set aside **silver** ...

Table 2: Examples and their judgements, with the last being debatable.

filtering out paraphrases that could have been retrieved as synonyms[11] from WordNet v3.0. The results of these experiments are in Table 3.

To evaluate the quality of our additional output over WordNet we assigned one of the following labels to 25 paraphrase sets generated at the end of Experiment 1b[12]: 1, the paraphrase (a) invoked the correct frame and (b) was grammatical; or 2, only (a) held; or 3, (a) did not hold. Table 4 presents aggregates over the labels.

PPDB	1a	1b	2a	2b
S	4,582	2,574	1,064,926	1,022,533
M	15,459	9,752	1,314,169	1,263,087
L	73,763	55,517	2,417,760	2,347,656
XL	340,406	283,126	–	–

Table 3: The total number of paraphrases generated for the 23,226 input targets versus different sizes of PPDB. The paraphrase count excludes the input. Column 1a and 2a represent unfiltered paraphrases as opposed to 1b and 2b where they have been filtered using WordNet v3.0.

PPDB Size	1	2	3	%(1+2)	%(1)
S	0	0	0	–	–
M	6	1	2	77.77	66.67
L	27	15	11	86.25	50.94
L rank 3	23	12	7	83.33	54.76
XL	110	85	50	79.60	44.89
XL rank 3	47	16	9	87.5	65.27
XL rank 5	69	28	13	88.18	62.72
XL rank 10	105	52	32	83.07	55.55

Table 4: Average quality of all paraphrases for 25 random sentences. Rows marked *A rank B* convey that we used PPDB of size *A* and kept only the top *B* sentences after sorting them by their language model score. Column %(1) indicates the percentage of output which was grammatical and evoked the correct frame. Column%(1+2) represents the output that evoked the correct frame.

4 Discussion And Conclusion

We presented initial experiments on using PPDB to automatically expand FrameNet through paraphrastic re-writing. We found that over a sample of 25 target words the top three paraphrases produced by PPDB XL evoked the correct frame and were grammatical 65% of the time.[13] However, work remains in recognizing the contexts in which a paraphrase is appropriately applied, and in improving the quality of PPDB itself.

Upon error analysis, we found two major reasons for ungrammaticality of lexical paraphrases. First: within FrameNet some sentences will have a single token annotated as trigger, when in fact it is part of a multi-word expression. For example, it was grammatically infelicitous to replace *part* by *portion* in the expression *part of the answer*. The other major source of error was the inaccuracy in PPDB itself. We found that for a large number of cases when PPDB XL did not have a high number of paraphrases the paraphrases were wrong (e.g., PPDB XL had only 2 paraphrases for the words *lab* and *millions*.)

Going forward we aim to increase the precision of our paraphrases and our ability to recognize their appropriate contexts for application. Further, we wish to augment additional resources in a similar way, for example PropBank or the ACE corpus (Walker et al., 2006). We should be able to increase the precision by using the paraphrase probability features of a PPDB rule and by using better language models with lower perplexity than n-grams e.g. recurrent neural net based language models. Improving the accuracy of PPDB, especially in the large settings, would be another focus area. Also, we would use Amazon Mechanical Turk to evaluate the quality of a larger set of paraphrases to make our evaluation robust and so that we can evaluate the efficacy of our second experiment.

Acknowledgments This material is based on research sponsored by the NSF under grant IIS-1249516 and DARPA under agreement number FA8750-13-2-0017.

[11] Two lemmas that appear in the same synset at least once are synonyms in our experiments.

[12] Experiment 2 generated significantly more candidates; here we consider only the potential scope of expansion and rely on Experiment 1 to gauge the likely paraphrase quality.

[13] We have released the generated corpus as well as the manual annotations at `cs.jhu.edu/~prastog3/res/fnppdb.html`

References

Roni Ben Aharon, Idan Szpektor, and Ido Dagan. 2010. Generating entailment rules from framenet. In *Proceedings of the ACL 2010 Conference Short Papers*, pages 241–246.

Collin Baker, Michael Ellsworth, and Katrin Erk. 2007. Semeval'07 task 19: frame semantic structure extraction. In *Proceedings of the 4th International Workshop on Semantic Evaluations*, pages 99–104. ACL.

Bob Coyne and Owen Rambow. 2009. Lexpar: A freely available english paraphrase lexicon automatically extracted from framenet. *2012 IEEE Sixth International Conference on Semantic Computing*, pages 53–58.

Dipanjan Das, Desai Chen, André F. T. Martins, Nathan Schneider, and Noah A. Smith. 2013. Frame-semantic parsing. *Computational Linguistics*, 40(1):9–56.

Oscar Ferrández, Michael Ellsworth, Rafael Munoz, and Collin F Baker. 2010. Aligning framenet and wordnet based on semantic neighborhoods. In *LREC*, volume 10, pages 310–314.

Charles J Fillmore and Collin F Baker. 2001. Frame semantics for text understanding. In *Proceedings of WordNet and Other Lexical Resources Workshop, NAACL*.

Marco Fossati, Claudio Giuliano, and Sara Tonelli. 2013. Outsourcing framenet to the crowd. In *Proceedings of the 51st Annual Meeting of the ACL*, pages 742–747.

Juri Ganitkevitch, Benjamin Van Durme, and Chris Callison-Burch. 2013. PPDB: The paraphrase database. In *Proceedings of NAACL-HLT*, pages 758–764, Atlanta, Georgia, June. ACL.

Daniel Gildea and Daniel Jurafsky. 2002. Automatic labeling of semantic roles. *Computational linguistics*, 28(3):245–288.

Kenneth Heafield, Ivan Pouzyrevsky, Jonathan H. Clark, and Philipp Koehn. 2013. Scalable modified Kneser-Ney language model estimation. In *Proceedings of the 51st Annual Meeting of the ACL*, Sofia, Bulgaria.

Jiří Materna. 2012. Lda-frames: An unsupervised approach to generating semantic frames. In *Computational Linguistics and Intelligent Text Processing*, volume 7181 of *Lecture Notes in Computer Science*, pages 376–387. Springer Berlin Heidelberg.

Courtney Napoles, Matthew Gormley, and Benjamin Van Durme. 2012. Annotated gigaword. In *Proceedings of the Joint Workshop on Automatic Knowledge Base Construction and Web-scale Knowledge Extraction*, pages 95–100. ACL.

Brendan O' Connor. 2012. Learning frames from text with an unsupervised latent variable model. In *Technical Report*. Carnegie Mellon University.

Jansen Orfan and James Allen. 2013. Toward learning high-level semantic frames from definitions. In *Proceedings of the Second Annual Conference on Advances in Cognitive Systems*, volume 125.

Martha Palmer, Daniel Gildea, and Paul Kingsbury. 2005. The proposition bank: An annotated corpus of semantic roles. *Computational Linguistics*, 31(1):71–106.

Rion Snow, Daniel Jurafsky, and Andrew Y Ng. 2004. Learning syntactic patterns for automatic hypernym discovery. In *NIPS*, volume 17, pages 1297–1304.

Christopher Walker, Stephanie Strassel, Julie Medero, and Kazuaki Maeda. 2006. Ace 2005 multilingual training corpus. *Linguistic Data Consortium, Philadelphia*.

Verbal Valency Frame Detection and Selection in Czech and English

Ondřej Dušek, Jan Hajič and **Zdeňka Urešová**
Charles University in Prague
Faculty of Mathematics and Physics
Institute of Formal and Applied Linguistics
Malostranské náměstí 25, 11800 Prague 1, Czech Republic
{odusek,hajic,uresova}@ufal.mff.cuni.cz

Abstract

We present a supervised learning method for verbal valency frame detection and selection, i.e., a specific kind of word sense disambiguation for verbs based on subcategorization information, which amounts to detecting mentions of events in text. We use the rich dependency annotation present in the Prague Dependency Treebanks for Czech and English, taking advantage of several analysis tools (taggers, parsers) developed on these datasets previously. The frame selection is based on manually created lexicons accompanying these treebanks, namely on PDT-Vallex for Czech and EngVallex for English. The results show that verbal predicate detection is easier for Czech, but in the subsequent frame selection task, better results have been achieved for English.

1 Introduction

Valency frames are a detailed semantic and syntactic description of individual predicate senses.[1] As such, they represent different event types. We present a system for automatic detection and selection of verbal valency frames in Czech and English, which corresponds to detecting and disambiguating mentions of events in text. This is an important step toward event instance identification, which should help greatly in linking the mentions of a single event. We took advantage of the fact that the Prague family of dependency treebanks contains comparable valency frame annotation for Czech and English (cf. Section 2). Thus the feature templates used in frame selection are the same and the features initially considered differ only in their instantiation (cf. Section 3).

While somewhat similar to the CoNLL 2009 Shared Task (Hajič et al., 2009) in the predicate detection part, our task differs from the semantic role labeling task in that the whole frame has to be detected, not only individual arguments, and is therefore more difficult not only in terms of scoring, but also in the selection part: several verbal frames might share the same syntactic features, making them virtually indistinguishable unless semantics is taken into account, combined with a detailed grammatical and morphological context.

2 Valency in the tectogrammatical description

The annotation scheme of the Prague Dependency Treebank (Bejček et al., 2012, PDT) and the Prague Czech-English Dependency Treebank (Hajič et al., 2012, PCEDT) is based on the formal framework of the Functional Generative Description (Sgall, 1967; Sgall et al., 1986, FGD), developed within the Prague School of Linguistics. The FGD is dependency-oriented with a "stratificational" (layered) approach to a systematic description of a language. The notion of valency in the FGD is one of the core concepts operating on the layer of linguistic meaning (*tectogrammatical layer, t-layer*).

2.1 Valency frames

The FGD uses syntactic as well as semantic criteria to identify verbal complements. It is assumed that all semantic verbs – and, potentially, nouns, adjectives, and adverbs – have subcategorization requirements, which can be specified in the *valency frame*.

Verbal valency modifications are specified along two axes: The first axis concerns the (general) opposition between inner participants (*arguments*) and free modifications (*adjuncts*). This dis-

[1] Valency can be observed for verbs, nouns, adjectives and in certain theories, also for other parts of speech; however, we focus on verbal valency only, as it is most common and sufficiently described in theory and annotated in treebanks.

Proceedings of the 2nd Workshop on EVENTS: Definition, Detection, Coreference, and Representation, pages 6–11, Baltimore, Maryland, USA, June 22-27, 2014.

tinction is based on criteria relating to:

(a) the possibility of the same type of complement appearing multiple times with the same verb (arguments cannot), and

(b) the possibility of the occurrence of the given complements (in principle) with any verb (typical for adjuncts).

The other axis relates to the distinction between (semantically) *obligatory* and *optional* complements of the word, which again is based on certain operational criteria expressed as the *dialogue test* (Panevová, 1974). Five arguments are distinguished: *Actor* (ACT), *Patient* (PAT), *Addressee* (ADDR), *Origin* (ORIG), and *Effect* (EFF). The set of free modifications is much larger than that of arguments; about 50 types of adjuncts are distinguished based on semantic criteria. Their set can be divided into several subclasses: temporal (e.g., TWHEN, TSIN), local (e.g., LOC, DIR3), causal (such as CAUS, CRIT), and other free modifications (e.g., MANN for general *Manner*, ACMP for *Accompaniment*, EXT for *Extent* etc.).

All arguments (obligatory or optional) and obligatory adjuncts are considered to be part of the valency frame.

2.2 Tectogrammatical annotation

The PDT is a project for FGD-based manual annotation of Czech texts, started in 1996 at the Institute of Formal and Applied Linguistics, Charles University in Prague. It serves two main purposes:

1. to test and validate the FGD linguistic theory,
2. to apply and test machine learning methods for part-of-speech and morphological tagging, dependency parsing, semantic role labeling, coreference resolution, discourse annotation, natural language generation, machine translation and other natural language processing tasks.

The language data in the PDT are non-abbreviated articles from Czech newspapers and journals.

The PCEDT contains English sentences from the Wall Street Journal section of the Penn Treebank (Marcus et al., 1993, PTB-WSJ) and their Czech translations, all annotated using the same theoretical framework as the PDT.

The annotation of the PDT and the PCEDT is very rich in linguistic information. Following the stratificational approach of the FGD, the texts are annotated at different but interlinked layers. There are four such layers, two linear and two structured:

- the word layer (*w-layer*) – tokenized but otherwise unanalyzed original text,
- the morphological layer (*m-layer*) with parts-of-speech, morphology and lemmatization,
- analytical layer (*a-layer*) – surface dependency syntax trees,
- tectogrammatical layer (*t-layer*) – "deep syntax" trees according to the FGD theory.

While the PDT has all the layers annotated manually, the PCEDT English annotation on the *a-layer* has been created by automatic conversion from the original Penn Treebank, including the usual head assignment; morphology and the tectogrammatical layer are annotated manually, even if not as richly as for Czech.[2]

Valency is a core ingredient on the t-layer. Since valency frames guide, i.a., the labeling of arguments, valency lexicons with sense-distinguished entries for both languages have been created to ensure consistent annotation.

2.3 Valency Lexicons for Czech and English in the FGD Framework

PDT-Vallex (Hajič et al., 2003; Urešová, 2011) is a valency lexicon of Czech verbs, nouns, and adjectives, created in a bottom-up way during the annotation of the PDT. This approach made it possible to confront the pre-existing valency theory with the real usage of the language.

Each entry in the lexicon contains a headword, according to which the valency frames are grouped, indexed, and sorted. Each valency frame includes the frame's "valency" (number of arguments, or frame members) and the following information for each argument:

- its label (see Section 2.1),
- its (semantic) obligatoriness according to Panevová (1974)'s dialogue test,
- its required surface form (or several alternative forms) typically using morphological, lexical and syntactic constraints.

Most valency frames are further accompanied by a note or an example which explains their meaning and usage. The version of PDT-Vallex used here contains 9,191 valency frames for 5,510 verbs.

EngVallex (Cinková, 2006) is a valency lexicon of English verbs based on the FGD framework, created by an automatic conversion from

[2]Attributes such as tense are annotated automatically, and most advanced information such as topic and focus annotation is not present.

PropBank frame files (Palmer et al., 2005) and by subsequent manual refinement.[3] EngVallex was used for the tectogrammatical annotation of the English part of the PCEDT. Currently, it contains 7,699 valency frames for 4,337 verbs.

3 Automatic frame selection

Building on the modules for Czech and English automatic tectogrammatical annotation used in the TectoMT translation engine (Žabokrtský et al., 2008) and the CzEng 1.0 corpus (Bojar et al., 2012),[4] we have implemented a system for automatic valency frame selection within the Treex NLP Framework (Popel and Žabokrtský, 2010).

The frame selection system is based on logistic regression from the LibLINEAR package (Fan et al., 2008). We use separate classification models for each verbal lemma showing multiple valency frames in the training data. Due to identical annotation schemata in both languages, our models use nearly the same feature set,[5] consisting of:

- the surface word form of the lexical verb and all its auxiliaries,
- their morphological attributes, such as part-of-speech and grammatical categories,
- formemes – compact symbolic morphosyntactic labels (e.g., `v:fin` for a finite verb, `v:because+fin` for a finite verb governed by a subordinating conjunction, `v:in+ger` for a gerund governed by a preposition),[6]
- syntactic labels given by the dependency parser,
- all of the above properties found in the topological and syntactic neighborhood of the verbal node on the *t-layer* (parent, children, siblings, nodes adjacent in the word order).

We experimented with various classifier settings (regularization type and cost C, termination criterion E) and feature selection techniques (these involve adding a subset of features according to a metric against the target class).[7]

4 Experiments

We evaluated the system described in Section 3 on PDT 2.5 for Czech and on the English part of PCEDT 2.0 for English. From PCEDT 2.0, whose division follows the PTB-WSJ, we used Sections 02-21 as training data, Section 24 as development data, and Section 23 as evaluation data. Since the system is intended to be used in a fully automatic annotation scenario, we use automatically parsed sentences with projected gold-standard valency frames to train the classifiers.

The results of our system in the best setting for both languages are given in Table 1.[8] The *unlabeled* figures measure the ability of the system to detect that a valency frame should be filled for a given node. The *labeled* figures show the overall system performance, including selecting the correct frame. The *frame selection accuracy* value shows only the percentage of frames selected correctly, disregarding misplaced frames. The accuracy for *ambiguous verbs* further disregards frames of lemmas where only one frame is possible. Here we include a comparison of our trained classifier with a baseline that always selects the most frequent frame seen in the training data.[9] Our results using the classifier for both languages have been confirmed by pairwise bootstrap resampling (Koehn, 2004) to be significantly better than the baseline at 99% level.

We can see that the system is more successful in Czech in determining whether a valency frame should be filled for a given node. This is most probably given by the fact that the most Czech verbs are easily recognizable by their morphological endings, whereas English verbs are more prone to be misrepresented as nouns or adjectives.

The English system is better at selecting the correct valency frame. This is probably caused by a more fine-grained word sense resolution in the Czech valency lexicon, where more figurative uses and idioms are included. For example, over 16%

[3] This process resulted in the interlinkage of both lexicons, with additional links to VerbNet (Schuler, 2005) where available. Due to the refinement, the mapping is often not 1:1.

[4] Note that annotation used in TectoMT and CzEng does not contain all attributes found in corpora manually annotated on the tectogrammatical layer. Valency frame IDs are an example of an attribute that is missing from the automatic annotation of CzEng 1.0.

[5] The only differences are due to the differences of part-of-speech tagsets used.

[6] See (Dušek et al., 2012; Rosa et al., 2012) for a detailed description of formemes.

[7] The metrics used include the Anova F-score, minimum Redundancy-Maximum Relevance (mRMR) (Peng et al., 2005), ReliefF (Kononenko, 1994), mutual information (MI), symmetric uncertainty (Witten and Frank, 2005, p. 291f.), and an average of the ranks given by mRMR and MI.

[8] The best setting for Czech uses L1-regularization and 10% best features according to Anova, with other parameters tuned on the development set for each lemma. The best setting for English uses L2-regularization with best feature subsets tuned on the development set and fixed parameters $C = 0.1$, $E = 0.01$.

[9] All other parts of the system, up to the identification of the frame to be filled in, are identical with the baseline.

		Czech	English
Unlabeled precision		99.09	96.03
Unlabeled recall		94.81	93.07
Unlabeled F-1		96.90	94.53
Labeled precision		78.38	81.58
Labeled recall		74.99	79.06
Labeled F-1		76.65	80.30
Frame selection accuracy		79.10	84.95
Ambiguous verbs	baseline	66.68	68.44
	classifier	72.41	80.03

Table 1: Experimental results

of errors in the Czech evaluation data were caused just by idioms or light verb constructions not being recognized by our system. In Czech, additional 15% of errors occurred for verbs where two or more valency frames share the same number of arguments and their labels, but these verb senses are considered different (because they have different meaning), compared to only 9% in English.

5 Related Work

As mentioned previously, the task of detecting and selecting valency frames overlaps with semantic role labeling (Hajič et al., 2009). However, there are substantial differences: we have focused only on verbs (as opposed to all words with some semantic relation marked in the data), and evaluated on the exact frame assigned to the occurrence of the verb in the treebank. On the other hand, we are also evaluating predicate identification as in Surdeanu et al. (2008), which Hajič et al. (2009) do not. Tagging and parsing have been automatic, but not performed jointly with the frame selection task. This also explains that while the best results reported for the CoNLL 2009 Shared task (Björkelund et al., 2009) are 85.41% labeled F-1 for Czech and 85.63% for English, they are not comparable due to several reasons, the main being that SRL evaluates each argument separately, while for a frame to be counted as correct in our task, the whole frame (by means of the reference ID) must be selected correctly, which is substantially harder (if only for verbs). Moreover, we have used the latest version of the PDT (the PDT 2.5), and EngVallex-annotated verbs in the PCEDT, while the English CoNLL 2009 Shared Task is PropBank-based.[10]

Selecting valency frames is also very similar to Word Sense Disambiguation (WSD), see e.g. (Edmonds and Cotton, 2001; Chen and Palmer, 2005). The WSD however does not consider subcategorization/valency information explicitly.

Previous works on the PDT include a rule-based tool of Honetschläger (2003) and experiments by Semecký (2007) using machine learning. Both of them, unlike our work, used gold-standard annotation with just the frame ID removed.

6 Conclusions

We have presented a method of detecting mentions of events in the form of verbal valency frame selection for Czech and English. This method is based on logistic regression with morphological and syntactic features, trained on treebanks with a comparable annotation scheme. We believe that these results are first for this task on the granularity of the lexicons (PDT-Vallex for Czech and EngVallex for English), and they seem to be encouraging given that the most frequent verbs like *to be* and *to have* have tens of possible frames, heavily weighing down the resulting scores.

We plan to extend this work to use additional features and lexical clustering, as well as to see if the distinctions in the lexicons are justified, i.e. if humans can effectively distinguish them in the first place, similar to the work of Cinková et al. (2012). A natural extension is to combine this work with argument labeling to match or improve on the "perfect proposition" score of Surdeanu et al. (2008) while still keeping the sense distinctions on top of it. We could also compare this to other languages for which similar valency lexicons exist, such as SALSA for German (Burchardt et al., 2006) or Chinese PropBank (Xue, 2008).

Acknowledgments

This work was supported by the Grant No. GPP406/13/03351P of the Grant Agency of the Czech Republic, the project LH12093 of the Ministry of Education, Youth and Sports of the Czech Republic and the Charles University SVV project 260 104. It has been using language resources developed, stored, and distributed by the LINDAT/CLARIN project of the Ministry of Education, Youth and Sports of the Czech Republic (project LM2010013).

[10]Please recall that EngVallex is a manually refined PropBank with different labeling scheme and generally $m : n$ mapping between PropBank and EngVallex frames.

References

E. Bejček, J. Panevová, J. Popelka, P. Straňák, M. Ševčíková, J. Štěpánek, and Z. Žabokrtský. 2012. Prague Dependency Treebank 2.5 – a revisited version of PDT 2.0. In *Proceedings of COLING 2012: Technical Papers*, Mumbai.

A. Björkelund, L. Hafdell, and P. Nugues. 2009. Multilingual semantic role labeling. In *Proceedings of the Thirteenth Conference on Computational Natural Language Learning (CoNLL 2009): Shared Task*, pages 43–48, Boulder, Colorado, United States, June.

O. Bojar, Z. Žabokrtský, O. Dušek, P. Galuščáková, M. Majliš, D. Mareček, J. Maršík, M. Novák, M. Popel, and A. Tamchyna. 2012. The joy of parallelism with CzEng 1.0. In *LREC*, page 3921–3928, Istanbul.

A. Burchardt, K. Erk, A. Frank, A. Kowalski, S. Padó, and M. Pinkal. 2006. The SALSA corpus: a German corpus resource for lexical semantics. In *Proceedings of the 5th International Conference on Language Resources and Evaluation (LREC-2006)*.

J. Chen and M. Palmer. 2005. Towards robust high performance word sense disambiguation of English verbs using rich linguistic features. In *Natural Language Processing–IJCNLP 2005*, pages 933–944. Springer.

S. Cinková, M. Holub, and V. Kríž. 2012. Managing uncertainty in semantic tagging. In *Proceedings of the 13th Conference of the European Chapter of the Association for Computational Linguistics*, pages 840–850. Association for Computational Linguistics.

S. Cinková. 2006. From PropBank to EngValLex: adapting the PropBank-Lexicon to the valency theory of the functional generative description. In *Proceedings of the fifth International conference on Language Resources and Evaluation (LREC 2006), Genova, Italy*.

O. Dušek, Z. Žabokrtský, M. Popel, M. Majliš, M. Novák, and D. Mareček. 2012. Formemes in English-Czech deep syntactic MT. In *Proceedings of the Seventh Workshop on Statistical Machine Translation*, page 267–274.

P. Edmonds and S. Cotton. 2001. Senseval-2: Overview. In *The Proceedings of the Second International Workshop on Evaluating Word Sense Disambiguation Systems*, SENSEVAL '01, pages 1–5, Stroudsburg, PA, USA. Association for Computational Linguistics.

R. E Fan, K. W Chang, C. J Hsieh, X. R Wang, and C. J Lin. 2008. LIBLINEAR: a library for large linear classification. *The Journal of Machine Learning Research*, 9:1871–1874.

J. Hajič, M. Ciaramita, R. Johansson, D. Kawahara, M. A. Martí, L. Màrquez, A. Meyers, J. Nivre, S. Padó, J. Štěpánek, P. Straňák, M. Surdeanu, N. Xue, and Y. Zhang. 2009. The CoNLL-2009 shared task: Syntactic and semantic dependencies in multiple languages. In *Proceedings of the 13th Conference on Computational Natural Language Learning (CoNLL-2009), June 4-5*, Boulder, Colorado, USA.

J. Hajič, E. Hajičová, J. Panevová, P. Sgall, O. Bojar, S. Cinková, E. Fučíková, M. Mikulová, P. Pajas, J. Popelka, J. Semecký, J. Šindlerová, J. Štěpánek, J. Toman, Z. Urešová, and Z. Žabokrtský. 2012. Announcing Prague Czech-English Dependency Treebank 2.0. In *Proceedings of LREC*, pages 3153–3160, Istanbul.

J. Hajič, J. Panevová, Z. Urešová, A. Bémová, V. Kolářová, and P. Pajas. 2003. PDT-VALLEX: creating a large-coverage valency lexicon for treebank annotation. In *Proceedings of The Second Workshop on Treebanks and Linguistic Theories*, volume 9, page 57–68.

V. Honetschläger. 2003. Using a Czech valency lexicon for annotation support. In *Text, Speech and Dialogue*, pages 120–125. Springer.

P. Koehn. 2004. Statistical significance tests for machine translation evaluation. In *Empirical Methods in Natural Language Processing*, pages 388–395.

I. Kononenko. 1994. Estimating attributes: Analysis and extensions of RELIEF. In *Machine Learning: ECML-94*, page 171–182.

M. P. Marcus, M. A. Marcinkiewicz, and B. Santorini. 1993. Building a large annotated corpus of English: The Penn Treebank. *Computational linguistics*, 19(2):330.

M. Palmer, D. Gildea, and P. Kingsbury. 2005. The proposition bank: An annotated corpus of semantic roles. *Computational Linguistics*, 31(1):71–106.

J. Panevová. 1974. On verbal frames in functional generative description. *Prague Bulletin of Mathematical Linguistics*, 22:3–40.

H. Peng, F. Long, and C. Ding. 2005. Feature selection based on mutual information: criteria of max-dependency, max-relevance, and min-redundancy. *IEEE Transactions on pattern analysis and machine intelligence*, page 1226–1238.

M. Popel and Z. Žabokrtský. 2010. TectoMT: modular NLP framework. *Advances in Natural Language Processing*, pages 293–304.

R. Rosa, D. Mareček, and O. Dušek. 2012. DEPFIX: a system for automatic correction of Czech MT outputs. In *Proceedings of the Seventh Workshop on Statistical Machine Translation*, page 362–368. Association for Computational Linguistics.

K. K. Schuler. 2005. *VerbNet: A Broad-Coverage, Comprehensive Verb Lexicon*. Ph.D. thesis, Univ. of Pennsylvania.

J. Semecký. 2007. Verb valency frames disambiguation. *The Prague Bulletin of Mathematical Linguistics*, (88):31–52.

P. Sgall, E. Hajičová, and J. Panevová. 1986. *The meaning of the sentence in its semantic and pragmatic aspects*. D. Reidel, Dordrecht.

P. Sgall. 1967. *Generativní popis jazyka a česká deklinace*. Academia, Praha.

M. Surdeanu, R. Johansson, A. Meyers, L. Màrquez, and J. Nivre. 2008. The CoNLL 2008 shared task on joint parsing of syntactic and semantic dependencies. In *CoNLL 2008: Proceedings of the Twelfth Conference on Computational Natural Language Learning*, pages 159–177, Manchester, England, August. Coling 2008 Organizing Committee.

Z. Urešová. 2011. *Valenční slovník Pražského závislostního korpusu (PDT-Vallex)*. Studies in Computational and Theoretical Linguistics. Ústav formální a aplikované lingvistiky, Praha, Czechia, ISBN 978-80-904571-1-9, 375 pp.

I. H. Witten and E. Frank. 2005. *Data Mining: Practical machine learning tools and techniques*. Morgan Kaufmann Pub, 2nd edition.

N. Xue. 2008. Labeling Chinese predicates with semantic roles. *Computational linguistics*, 34(2):225–255.

Z. Žabokrtský, J. Ptáček, and P. Pajas. 2008. TectoMT: highly modular MT system with tectogrammatics used as transfer layer. In *Proceedings of the Third Workshop on Statistical Machine Translation*, page 167–170. Association for Computational Linguistics.

Challenges of Adding Causation to Richer Event Descriptions

Rei Ikuta[*], **William F. Styler IV**[+], **Mariah Hamang**[*], **Tim O'Gorman**[*], **and Martha Palmer**[*]
Department of Linguistics, University of Colorado at Boulder
[*]{rei.ikuta, mariah.hamang, ogormant, martha.palmer}@colorado.edu,
[+]will@savethevowels.org

Abstract

The goal of this study is to create guidelines for annotating cause-effect relations as part of the Richer Event Description schema. We present the challenges faced using the definition of causation in terms of counterfactual dependence and propose new guidelines for cause-effect annotation using an alternative definition which treats causation as an intrinsic relation between events. To support the use of such an intrinsic definition, we examine the theoretical problems that the counterfactual definition faces, show how the intrinsic definition solves those problems, and explain how the intrinsic definition adheres to psychological reality, at least for our annotation purposes, better than the counterfactual definition. We then evaluate the new guidelines by presenting results obtained from pilot annotations of ten documents, showing that an inter-annotator agreement (F1-score) of 0.5753 was achieved. The results provide a benchmark for future studies concerning cause-effect annotation in the RED schema.

1 Introduction: The RED schema and cause-effect relation

Richer Event Description (Styler et al., 2014a) is an annotation schema which is developed "as a synthesis of the THYME-TimeML guidelines[1], the Stanford Event coreference guidelines and the Carnegie Mellon University Event coreference guidelines." In other words, it combines Coreference (Pradhan et al., 2007; Lee et al. , 2012) and THYME Temporal Relations annotation (Styler et al. (2014b)) to provide a thorough representation of entities (including events) and their relations, including temporal relations. An overview of the annotation process, which shows how coreference and temporal annotations are combined, is described in the following section.

The RED schema therefore attempts to annotate cause-effect relations, which are annotated in neither Coreference nor THYME (Styler et al., 2014b). There is a synergy between annotating both causal and temporal relations, since causes necessarily precede their effects.

Other characteristics of the cause-effect annotation in RED are that it allows annotators to make inferences without relying on explicit connectives or verbs of causation, that it is not domain specific, and that it allows the relation to cross one (but not more than one) sentence boundary.

1.1 The annotation process

The process of RED annotation is divided into two passes: the first in which entities (including events) are annotated, and the second in which relations between those entities are annotated.

In the first pass, annotators identify three types of entities: events (an occurence with a definitive temporal duration), temporal expressions such as *August 2013*, and other entities that have an existence as opposed to an occurrence (e.g., proper nouns, objects, and pronouns). Specific properties of each event are also annotated in this pass (e.g., its relation to the document creation time, whether it is an actual event or a hypothetical event, etc.).

After the annotations in the first pass have been adjudicated, annotators mark temporal, cause-effect, and coreference relations between the entities identified in the first pass. Temporal relations (e.g., *before*, *overlaps*, *contains*) are annotated between two events or between an event and a TIMEX3, cause-effect relations are annotated between two events, and coreference relations are

[1] The THYME annotation schema also includes coreference annotation.

Proceedings of the 2nd Workshop on EVENTS: Definition, Detection, Coreference, and Representation, pages 12–20,
Baltimore, Maryland, USA, June 22-27, 2014.

annotated between two entities (e.g., *President John F. Kennedy ... he*) or two events (*an earthquake ... the quake*). Coreference relations include part-whole and set-member relations, as well as identical relations in which two entities share a referent.

As a result of combining Coreference and THYME, different coreference and temporal relations between an event pair can be covered by a single relation in RED. For example, a part-whole relation between events annotated in Coreference (e.g., *an incision* and *a surgury*) is a subset of temporal "contains" relation in RED.

Therefore, the goal of RED is to combine Coreference and THYME annotation, while finding overlaps between the two and also introducing cause-effect annotation to achieve a richer representation of entities, events, and their relations.

1.2 Overview of the following sections

In the following sections, we present the challenges faced during our first pilot annotation and why we decided to change the definition of causation, from a counterfactual one to an intrinsic one. To support the use of the intrinsic definition, we examine the theoretical problems that the counterfactual definition faces, show how the intrinsic definition solves those problems, and explain how the intrinsic definition adheres to psychological reality, at least for our annotation purposes, better than the counterfactual definition. We then propose new guidelines based on the intrinsic definition and evaluate them by presenting results obtained from our second pilot annotations of ten documents, showing that an inter-annotator agreement (F1-score) of 0.5753 was achieved.

2 Challenges of cause-effect annotation using the counterfactual definition

The pilot annotations were done by three annotators who are native speakers of English and are experienced in linguistic annotation, on English proxy reports (i.e., approximations of intelligence agency reports) written by Garland, et al. (2013).

Our original guidelines were based on the counterfactual definition of causation, as defined below. Early on in the annotation process, the cause-effect annotation was halted and removed from the RED schema because there were a number of cases in which events matched our guidelines for the cause-effect relation but did not match our intuitions about the relation.

2.1 Counterfactual definition of causation

In the original guidelines for cause-effect relations, we defined causation as follows:

- "X caused Y" means if X had not occurred, Y would not have occurred.

This definition of causation in terms of counterfactual dependence (as philosophers call it) has been the most popular definition of causation in the field of philosophy for the past forty years since David Lewis's possible world model (Lewis, 1973) and remain influential in contemporary studies such as the structural model (Pearl, 2000; Halpern and Pearl, 2005).

Using this definition, one annotator marked two causal relations between the two event pairs in the following sentence[2]:

> (1) PYONGYANG INSISTS IT WILL **ALLOW** FULL IAEA **INSPECTIONS** ONLY WHEN A SIGNIFICANT PORTION OF THE **PROJECT** AS **DEFINED** IN THE 1994 ACCORD IS COMPLETED.
>
> Annotations:
>
> **ALLOW** causes **INSPECTIONS**
>
> **DEFINED** causes **PROJECT**

These annotations are done perfectly in line with the guidelines[3], since there would be no *inspections* if there were no *allowing*, and there would be no *projects* if there were no *defining* (of the project). Furthermore, one could argue that the *1994 accord* causes Pyongyang to *insist*, since if there had been no such accord, Pyongyang would not have been able to insist anything pertaining to it, although the annotators did refrain from creating such a causal annotation.

However, the relation between these event pairs does not match our intuition about what causation is. For example, the *allowing* should be considered as a precondition for the *inspections*, and not

[2]Another annotator who annotated the same text did not mark any causal relations in this sentence.

[3]The annotation guidelines allow future events to be in causal relations, although the counterfactual definition only deals with past events, and for quoted speech, narrators are assumed to be reliable. Thus, future events can participate in a causal relation if the narrator is certain about the relation. If the relation is presented to be likely or hypothetical instead of being actual, annotators can mark such modalities also.

the cause. Furthermore, the guideline creates too many event pairs that are potentially in a cause-effect relation (such as the *accord* and the *insisting*), contributing to confusion among annotators.

A similar issue can be seen in the following sentence, in which *the internet* should be considered as a possible precondition of *funding*, and not the cause:

> (2) THE WORKSHOP WILL STUDY THE USE OF THE INTERNET TO PROMOTE TERRORISM AND THE **INTERNET'S** ROLE IN FACILITATING MONEY TRANSACTIONS AND **FUNDING** TERRORIST GROUPS.
>
> Annotation:
>
> **INTERNET'S** causes **FUNDING**

Therefore, we concluded that the counterfactual definition of causation is not optimal for our annotation guidelines, and that we need an alternative definition of causation which does not rely on annotators to consider a possible world in which the cause does not occur.

Such an alternative definition, which we call the intrinsic definition, has been argued for by Menzies (1996; 1999; 2014). Such a definition treats causation as an intrinsic relation between events, meaning that it is "a local relation depending on the intrinsic properties of the events and what goes on between them, and nothing else" (Menzies, 2014).

Drawing on Menzies idea, we propose the following definition of causation which is being used in our new guidelines for cause-effect annotation:

- "X caused Y" means Y was inevitable given X.

With this definition, annotators would not have to consider any possible worlds in which an event did not occur in order to annotate cause-effect relations, and only have to focus on whether Y necessarily follows X, according to the context and their encyclopedic knowledge of the world.

In order to support our use of such a definition, we also present the challenges that the counterfactual definition faces in terms of theory and psychological reality in the following sections, and show how the intrinsic definition solves those problems.

3 Theoretical challenge of the counterfactual definition

The two situations below illustrate theoretical challenges which are faced by the counterfactual definition but not by the intrinsic definition.

3.1 Multiple causes

- There are three events (1, 2 and 3), and three individuals (A, B, and C). Events 1 and 2 occur at the same time, and event 3 follows events 1 and 2.
- In event 1, A shoots C in the head.
- In event 2, B shoots C in the heart.
- In event 3, C dies.
- Then, an autopsy reveals that each of the shots C received (one in the head, shot by A, and the other in the heart, shot by B) was sufficient by itself to kill C.

In the above situation (a modified version of the example in Lagnado et al. (2013)), the counterfactual definition would falsely predict that both events 1 and 2 are not the causes of event 3, since even if event 1 did not occur, event 3 would have occurred because of event 2, and if event 2 did not occur, event 3 would have occurred because of event 1.

Acknowledging this problem, Halpern and Pearl (2005) retain the counterfactual notion and extend their causal model by stating that counterfactual dependence should be evaluated relative to certain contingencies. According to this definition, the counterfactual dependence of event 1 to event 3 should be evaluated relative to a contingency in which event 2 does not occur. The obvious problem that this extended model faces is the difficulty of finding a principled way to decide which contingencies are allowed. Although Halpern and Pearl (2005) do offer a complex set of conditions that are aimed at capturing the intuition that one should only invoke contingencies "that do not interfere with active causal processes," the question of which contingencies are allowed is non-trivial and is the subject of ongoing debate (Halpern and Hitchcock, 2010; Hiddleston, 2005; Hopkins and Pearl, 2003; Lagnado et al., 2013).

This situation, however, is easily handled by the intrinsic definition, since event 3 (the death of C) is inevitable given event 1 (A shooting C in the head) regardless of other events, and event 3 is inevitable given event 2 (B shooting C in the heart) regardless of other events, according to what we know about the results of the autopsy. Thus the intrinsic definition correctly predicts that both events 1 and 2 are equally the causes of event 3.

3.2 Oxygen, lightning, and wildfire

- There are three events (1, 2 and 3). Event 1 is a state encompassing events 2 and 3, and event 3 follows event 2.
- In event 1, oxygen exists.
- In event 2, a lightning strikes a tree in a forest.
- In event 3, a wildfire starts in the forest.

In this situation described by Halpern and Hitchcock (2013), event 1 (the existence of oxygen) would be predicted as being one of the causes of event 3 (wildfire), since if oxygen did not exist, a wildfire would not start. However, they argue that human intuition would treat only event 2, and not event 1, as a cause of event 3.

To counter this problem, Halpern and Hitchcock (2013) again extend the counterfactual model, stating that potential causes are graded according to the *normality* of their *witnesses* (a witness is a world in which a potential cause is the actual cause of an outcome). In this extended model, the world in which oxygen exists is more *normal* than the world in which lightning strikes a particular tree. Therefore, the lightning, being less normal, "receives a higher causal grading." In their causal model, a static ranking of the witnesses are given before the processing (i.e., causal inference) starts, and thus it is possible to compute which witness receives a higher causal grading.

Unlike the extended counterfactual definition, the intrinsic definition does not assume a given ranking of the world, and thus it is especially useful when applied to annotation tasks. For example, annotators would identify a causal relation between the oxygenation and the wildfire in the following sentence:

> (3) The **oxygenation** of the atmosphere accompanied by a lightning **strike** triggered the first **wildfire** in Earth's history.

But not in the following:

> (4) The first **wildfire** in Earth's history was caused by a lightning **strike** in the Proterozoic, an era noted for the evolution of multicellular organisms, glaciations, and the **oxygenation** of the atmosphere.

Even though the two events (*oxygenation* and *wildfire*) described in the above sentences refer to the same events in the world, the annotators can choose whether to note a causal link between them depending on the inevitability implied by the text. In sentence (2), it is suggested that the *wildfire* was inevitable given the *oxygenation* and the *strike*, thus both of the events would be annotated as the cause, while sentence (3) does not imply such a causal relation. This would effectively let the annotators avoid marking cause-effect relations between births and deaths in texts such as obituaries and medical reports. Such varying interpretations of texts are not possible with the original counterfactual definition, or with Halpern and Hitchcocks extended counterfactual model (2013) which assumes a given ranking of witnesses which is available to the writer but not to the annotator.

4 Challenge of the counterfactual definition in terms of psychological reality

In addition to the theoretical problem that the counterfactual definition faces, experiments done by White (2006) have shown that counterfactual dependence is not used as preferred evidence for making causal inference when subjects are passively (i.e., without the ability to intervene) exposed to a scenario in which there are a number of events affecting one another.

In one of the experiments, subjects are presented with scenarios concerning two game reserves, in each of which live five species, who may or may not prey on each other. For each reserve, there are five statements corresponding to five consecutive seasons, and each statement describes whether the population of each of the species has changed in that season. Based on the statements, the subjects must decide whether a change in the population of one species causes changes in that of the others. The subjects are instructed that if the population of X changed and that of Y did not in a given season, they are supposed to conclude that X does not prey on Y, because if it did, the populations of both X and Y would have changed.

In other words, the subjects are explicitly told to rely on counterfactual dependence as evidence for making causal inference. The five statements provided enough counterfactually dependent relations for the subjects to reach one correct answer.

However, the results of the experiment show that only 5 out of 36 subjects made correct judgments on the predator-prey (cause-effect) relations in both reserves, and the success rates were below optimum and not far above chance. Instead, the answers by the subjects showed that they were more likely to rely on the temporal order of events as the evidence for the causal relations (i.e., "the population of X changed in season 1 and that of Y changed in season 2, thus X must be the predator of Y"), although they were instructed to rely on counterfactual dependence within the same season instead.

White (2006) carried out three additional experiments, one in which he changed the order of the seasons, another in which subjects were told that the seasons were in random order and that the temporal order is irrelevant to the answer, and the last in which the scenario was changed to a situation where the levels of five chemicals in a blood stream affect each other. The subjects' answers exhibited more reliance on counterfactual dependence in the experiment where they were told that temporal order is irrelevant, but the other experiments showed similar results with the first experiment.

Thus, White (2006) concludes that there is a preference for basing causal inference on domain-specific causal knowledge (i.e., "the population change in season 1 must be causally related to the change in season 2, according to what we know about ecosystems") over counterfactual dependence, when such knowledge is available for use and when subjects are passively exposed[4] to a complex scenario in which there are a number of events affecting one another.

These results support our motivation to avoid using the counterfactual definition, since annotators are passively exposed to text without the ability to intervene, texts to be annotated are complex systems in which a number of events may or may not affect each other, and it is usually the case that domain-specific causal knowledge is available. The use of an intrinsic definition for cause-effect annotation, on the other hand, is in line with the results of these experiments, since annotators would not have to consider any possible worlds where some event does not occur, and only have to focus on whether Y necessarily follows X, according to the context and their encyclopedic knowledge of the world.

5 The new guidelines

Given the challenges faced by the counterfactual definition and the advantages of the intrinsic definition presented above, we developed new guidelines for cause-effect annotation which instruct annotators as follows:

- In our schema, we annotate "X CAUSES Y" if, according to the writer, the particular EVENT Y was inevitable given the particular EVENT X.

We then utilized the counterfactual definition as the definition of precondition relations as follows:

- We annotate "X PRECONDITIONS Y" if, according to the writer, had the particular EVENT X not happened, the particular EVENT Y would not have happened.

The reason we kept the counterfactual definition in our guidelines as a definition of a precondition relation is that the relation defined by counterfactual dependence still gives us information about the temporal relation between events; if we know that Y would not have happened if X had not happened, we also know that X started before Y.

6 The second pilot annotation

Using the new guidelines, ten proxy reports were each annotated by two annotators. One of them was among the two annotators who participated in our first pilot annotation, and the other, who is also a native speaker of English experienced in linguistic annotation, was trained using the old guidelines but only started annotating in the RED schema after the cause-effect annotation was halted, and thus had not actually annotated cause-effect relations until the second pilot. The following sections present the inter-annotator agreement of cause and precondition annotations done in the ten reports and the analysis of specific examples where the annotators disagreed.

[4]It has been claimed that subjects perform better in making causal inferences on complex structures when they are actively exposed to (i.e., have the ability to intervene with) the structures (Lagnado and Sloman, 2004; Sloman and Lagnado, 2005; Steyvers et al., 2003).

6.1 Inter-annotator agreement

This section presents the inter-annotator agreement (IAA) obtained from the second pilot annotation, and analyzes the annotations to examine the sources of disagreement between the annotators. Perhaps the most important thing to note before discussing the specific numbers and examples is that this pilot annotation did not include the adjudication stage between the first pass where entities including events and temporal expressions are identified, and the second pass where the relations between those entities are marked (see Section 1.1 for the specifics of the annotation process). Therefore, many of the disagreements in the causation and precondition annotations involve disagreements in the first pass.

A total of 114 relations (50 causation and 64 precondition relations) were created by the two annotators. Among them, 24 exhibited perfect match between the annotators, while 18 exhibited partial match (meaning that they agreed on whether the relation was causation/precondition, but disagreed on other aspects of the relation, such as the modality and temporal relation[5]) . Among the 114 relations, 72 relations showed disagreements, but 69 of them involved disagreements in the first pass. Upon analysis, we judged 41 of those 69 disagreements as being avoidable by introducing the adjudication stage between the two passes, and 28 as having the potential of surviving adjudication, meaning that even if the adjudication were properly done, the same parts of the text may still cause similar disagreements. Only 3 among the 72 disagreements occurred purely in the second pass, meaning that the annotators completely agreed on what the entities involved in the 3 relations should be, but disagreed on the relation.

Thus, the results give us four types of IAA (best-case, realistic, worst-case, and extra-strict), shown in Table 1 as F1-scores.

The best-case IAA assumes that all disagreements involving disagreements in the first pass will not show up as issues in the second pass, and only takes into account the 3 disagreements that occurred purely in the second pass.

	F1-score
Best-case	0.9333
Realistic	0.5753
Worst-case	0.3684
Extra-strict	0.2105

Table 1: Inter-annotator agreement for the second pilot annotation

The realistic IAA takes into account the 28 disagreements involving disagreements in the first pass that have the potential of surviving adjudication.

The worst-case IAA assumes that all disagreements in the first pass survive adjudication.

Finally, the extra-strict IAA allows relations to be judged as agreeing only when the two annotations completely match, including the modality and the temporal relations marked together with causation/precondition.

6.2 Evaluation of the inter-annotator agreement

This section compares the IAA presented above with results shown in a previous study by Styler et al. (2014b) which deals with temporal relation annotations in the clinical domain. In their study, Styler et al (2014b) reported results from annotations done on a subset of the THYME colon cancer corpus, which includes clinical notes and pathology reports for 35 patients diagnosed with colon cancer for a total of 107 documents. Two graduate or undergraduate students in the Department of Linguistics at the University of Colorado annotated each text. For the annotation guidelines, they used the THYME-TimeML guidelines which are also used within the RED guidelines for temporal relation annotation. Unlike the annotations in this current study, the temporal relation annotations on the THYME corpus were done after the identification of events and temporal expressions were adjudicated (the THYME-TimeML schema does not identify entities that are not events or temporal expressions). Therefore, the IAA they presented (Table 2) are not affected by the disagreements at the level of event identification.

The figure for "participants only" shows the IAA concerning cases in which the annotators

[5]As well as marking the modality (whether the relation is stated as being actual, likely or hypothetical) and the temporal relation (whether the cause ends before the effect starts or cause overlaps with the effect), annotators have a choice of marking a relation as "difficult" when they are not sure of their annotation. This difficulty marking was not considered when judging whether the two annotators agreed completely or not. In other words, even if one annotator marked a relation as difficult and the other did not, the annotation would be considered as showing complete agreement as long as other properties of the annotation matched.

	F1-score
Participants only	0.5012
Participants and relation	0.4506
"Contains" relaion	0.5630

Table 2: Inter-annotator agreement presented in Styler et al. (2014b)

agreed that there is some sort of a temporal relation between the two participants, but did not necessarily agree on which temporal relation (*before*, *overlap*, *contains*, etc.) holds between them. The figure for "participants and relation" shows the agreement on both the participants and the type of the temporal relation. The third figure is the IAA for the temporal relation "contains," which exhibited the highest IAA among all the temporal relations.

These figures are significantly higher than the results reported for the 2012 i2b2 challenge (Sun et al., 2013), in which the F1-score for "participants only" IAA was 0.39.

The realistic IAA of 0.5753 obtained in this current study is not far-off from the figures by Styler et al. (2014b), which shows that causation and precondition annotations using the new guidelines are indeed feasible.

6.3 Examples of disagreements

Below, we present examples of different types of disagreements observed in the annotations. The annotations are represented in the form of "EVENT relation-relation EVENT." The first half of the relation indicates the temporal relation annotated between the events, and the latter half shows whether there was a causation or a precondition relation between the events. For example, "P before-cause Q" indicates that event P happened before and caused event Q.

6.3.1 Disagreement in the 1st pass: avoidable by adjudication

(5) A **BUDGET** WAS **ALLOCATED** FOR THE BARRIER TO BE **EQUIPPED** WITH ELECTRONIC DETENTION EQUIPMENT.

Annotations by annotators X and Y:
X: **ALLOCATED** before-preconditions **EQUIPPED**

Y: **BUDGET** before-preconditions **EQUIPPED**

In (5), annotator X marked *allocated* as an event while not marking *budget* as an event, and Y annotated *budget* as an event and did not mark *allocated* as an event. If the adjudication was correctly done, only marking *allocated* as an event and not *budget*, it is likely that Y would have annotated the same way as X.

6.3.2 Disagreement in the 1st pass: not avoidable by adjudication

(6) CRITICS STATE THAT WITH ACCESS TO PLUTONIUM AVAILABLE FROM ROGUE STATES TERRORISTS COULD **CONSULT** THE DETAILED DOCUMENTS AND **BUILD** AN ATOMIC BOMB.

Y: **CONSULT** before-preconditions **BUILD**

X: No relations identified

In (6), the annotators did disagree on whether the two events *consult* and *build* happen after or overlap with the document creation time (DocTime). X annotated those two events as overlapping the DocTime, while Y annotated them as after the DocTime. The annotators agreed that those two events were hypothetical events. Although such a disagreement about the temporal property of the events may have caused the disagreements about whether there should be a precondition relation, it is likely that X would have missed what Y had found even if there had been adjudication.

6.3.3 Disagreements in the 2nd pass

(7) THE SMH AND JENNINGS WERE THEN **SUED** OVER 3 ARTICLES **PUBLISHED** IN THE LEAD-UP TO THE 000000 OLYMPICS.

X: No relations identified

Y: **PUBLISHED** before-preconditions **SUED**

(8) HEAD OF A TAJIK GOVERNMENT AGENCY THAT FIGHTS DRUG TRAFFICKING AVAZ YULDACHEV STATED THAT HEROIN USERS ARE **ILL** AND **NEED** TREATMENT.

X: **ILL** overlap-cause **NEED**

Y: No relations identified

(7) and (8) above show cases in which one annotator missed the relation that the other annotator identified, even though both annotators completely agreed on the property of the entities involved in the relation.

7 Conclusion

In this paper, we have presented the challenges that the counterfactual definition of causation faces in terms of its application to annotation guidelines, theory, and psychological reality. We have shown that the intrinsic definition better suits our purpose of annotation, and proposed new guidelines for annotating cause-effect relations using such a definition. The new guidelines were evaluated using results obtained from a pilot annotation of ten documents. An inter-annotator agreement (F1-score) of 0.5753 was obtained. We are currently in the process of training four additional annotators with the new guidelines, and future studies concerning cause-effect annotation in the RED schema can assess their performances by using results presented in this paper as a benchmark.

Acknowledgments

The project described was supported by DARPA FA-8750-13-2-0045, subaward 560215 (via LDC) DEFT: Deep Exploration and Filtering of Text and NIH: 1 R01 LM010090-01A1, THYME (via Harvard). The content is solely the responsibility of the authors and does not necessarily represent the official views of DARPA or NIH.

References

Garland, J., Fore, D., Strassel, S., and Grimes, S. 2013. *DEFT Phase 1 Narrative Text Source Data R1 LDC2013E19*. Web download file. Philadelphia: Linguistic Data Consortium

Halpern, J. Y., and Hitchcock, C. 2010. Actual causation and the art of modeling. In R. Dechter, H. Geffner,and J. Y. Halpern, eds., *Heuristics, probability and causality: A Tribute to Judea Pearl.* (pp. 383–406). London: College Publications.

Halpern, J. Y., and Hitchcock, C. 2013. Compact Representations of Extended Causal Models. *Cognitive Science*, 37:986–1010.

Halpern, J. Y., and Pearl, J. 2005. Causes and explanations: A structural-model approach. Part I: Causes. *The British Journal for the Philosophy of Science*, 56(4):843–887.

Hiddleston, E. 2005. A causal theory of counterfactuals. *Nous*, 39(4):632–657.

Hopkins, M., and Pearl, J. 2003. Clarifying the usage of structural models for commonsense causal reasoning. In P. Doherty, J. McCarthy, M. Williams, eds., *Proceedings of the AAAI Spring Symposium on Logical Formalization of Commonsense Rea-soning*. (pp. 83–89). Menlo Park, CA: AAAI Press.

Knobe, J., and Fraser, B. 2008. Causal judgment and moral judgment: Two experiments. In W. Sinnott-Armstrong, eds., *Moral psychology, Volume 2: The cognitive science of morality*. (pp. 441–447). Cambridge, MA: MIT Press.

Lagnado, D. A., Gerstenburg, T., and Zultan, R. 2013. Causal Responsibility and Counterfactuals. *Cognitive Science* 37:1036–1073.

Lagnado, D. A., and Sloman, S. 2004. The advantage of timely intervention. *Journal of Experimental Psychology: Learning, Memory and Cognition*, 30:856–876.

Lee, H., Recasens, M., Chang, A., Surdeanu, M., and Jurafsky, D. 2012. Joint entity and event coreference resolution across documents. In *Proceedings of the Conference on Empirical Methods in Natural Language Processing and Computational Natural Language Learning (EMNLP-CoNLL)*, Jeju Island, 489-500.

Lewis, D. 1973. Causation. *The Journal of Philosophy*, 70(17):556–567.

Menzies, P. 1996. Probabilistic Causation and the Preemption Problem. *Mind*, 105:85–117.

Menzies, P. 1999. Intrinsic versus Extrinsic Conceptions of Causation. In H. Sankey, ed., *Causation and Laws of Nature*, Kluwer Academic Publishers, pp. 313–29.

Menzies, P. 2014. Counterfactual Theories of Causation. In E. N. Zalta, ed., *The Stanford Encyclopedia of Philosophy*. Retrieved from `http://plato.stanford.edu/archives/spr2014/entries/causation-counterfactual/`

Pearl, J. 2000. *Causality*. Cambridge: Cambridge University Press.

Pradhan, S. Ramshaw, L., Weischedel, R., MacBride, J., and Micciulla, L. 2007. Unrestricted Coreference: Indentifying Entities and Events in OntoNotes. In *Proceedings of the IEEE International Conference on Semantic Computing (ICSC)*, September 17-19.

Sloman, S., and Lagnado, D. A. 2005. Do we "do"? *Cognitive Science*, 29:5–39.

Steyvers, M., Tenenbaum, J. T., Wagenmakers, E. J., and Blum, B. 2003. Inferring causal networks from observations and interventions. em Cognitive Science, 27:453–489.

Styler, W., Crooks, K., O'Gorman, T., and Hamang, M. 2014a. *Richer Event Description (RED) Annotation Guidelines.* Unpublished manuscript, University of Colorado at Boulder.

Styler, W. F., Bethard, S., Finan, S., Palmer, M., Pradhan, S., de Groen, P. C., Erickson, B., Miller, T., Lin, C., Savova, G., and Pustejovsky., J. 2014b. Temporal Annotation in the Clinical Domain, *Transactions of the Association of Computational Linguistics*, 2:143–154.

White, P. A. 2006. How well is causal structure inferred from cooccurrence information? *European Journal of Cognitive Psychology*, 18 (3):454–480.

Inter-Annotator Agreement for ERE Annotation

Seth Kulick and **Ann Bies** and **Justin Mott**
Linguistic Data Consortium, University of Pennsylvania, Philadelphia, PA 19104
{skulick,bies,jmott}@ldc.upenn.edu

Abstract

This paper describes a system for inter-annotator agreement analysis of ERE annotation, focusing on entity mentions and how the higher-order annotations such as EVENTS are dependent on those entity mentions. The goal of this approach is to provide both (1) quantitative scores for the various levels of annotation, and (2) information about the types of annotation inconsistencies that might exist. While primarily designed for inter-annotator agreement, it can also be considered a system for evaluation of ERE annotation.

1 Introduction

In this paper we describe a system for analyzing dually human-annotated files of Entities, Relations, and Events (ERE) annotation for consistency between the two files. This is an important aspect of training new annotators, to evaluate the consistency of their annotation with a "gold" file, or to evaluate the agreement between two annotators. We refer to both cases here as the task of "inter-annotator agreement" (IAA).

The light ERE annotation task was defined as part of the DARPA DEFT program (LDC, 2014a; LDC, 2014b; LDC, 2014c) as a simpler version of tasks like ACE (Doddington et al., 2004) to allow quick annotation of a simplified ontology of entities, relations, and events, along with identity coreference. The ENTITIES consist of co-referenced entity mentions, which refer to a span of text in the source file. The entity mentions are also used as part of the annotation of RELATIONS and EVENTS, as a stand in for the whole ENTITY.

The ACE program had a scoring metric described in (Doddington et al., 2004). However, our emphasis for IAA evaluation is somewhat different than that of scoring annotation files for accuracy with regard to a gold standard. The IAA system aims to produce output to help an annotation manager understand the sorts of errors occurring, and the general range of possible problems. Nevertheless, the approach to IAA evaluation described here can be used for scoring as well. This approach is inspired by the IAA work for treebanks in Kulick et al. (2013).

Because the entity mentions in ERE are the fundamental units used for the ENTITY, EVENT and RELATION annotations, they are also the fundamental units upon which the IAA evaluation is based. The description of the system therefore begins with a focus on the evaluation of the consistency of the entity mention annotations. We derive a mapping between the entity mentions between the two files (henceforth called File A and File B). We then move on to ENTITIES, RELATIONS, and EVENTS, pointing out the differences between them for purposes of evaluation, but also their similarities.[1]

This is a first towards a more accurate use of the full ENTITIES in the comparison and scoring of ENTITIES and EVENTS annotations. Work to expand in this direction is in progress. When a more complete system is in place it will be more appropriate to report corpus-based results.

2 Entity Mentions

There are two main aspects to the system's handling of entity mentions. First we describe the mapping of entity mentions between the two annotators. As in Doddington et al. (2004), the possibility of overlapping mentions can make this a complex problem. Second, we describe how our system's output categorizes possible errors.

[1]This short paper focuses on the design of the IAA system, rather than reporting on the results for a specific dataset. The IAA system has been run on dually annotated ERE data, however, which was the source for the examples in this paper.

Proceedings of the 2nd Workshop on EVENTS: Definition, Detection, Coreference, and Representation, pages 21–25,
Baltimore, Maryland, USA, June 22-27, 2014.

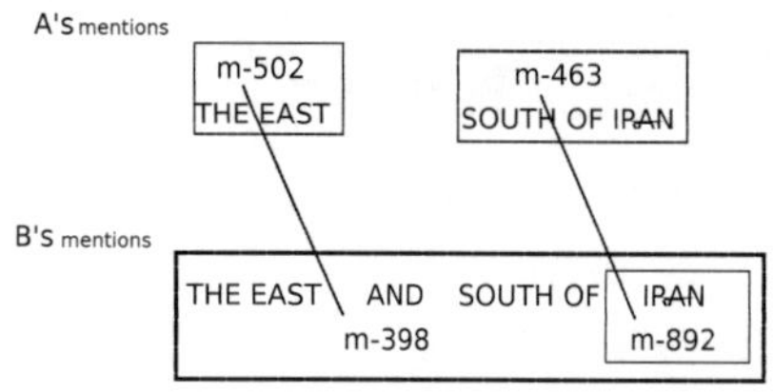

Figure 1: Case of ambiguous Entity Mention mapping disambiguated by another unambiguous mapping

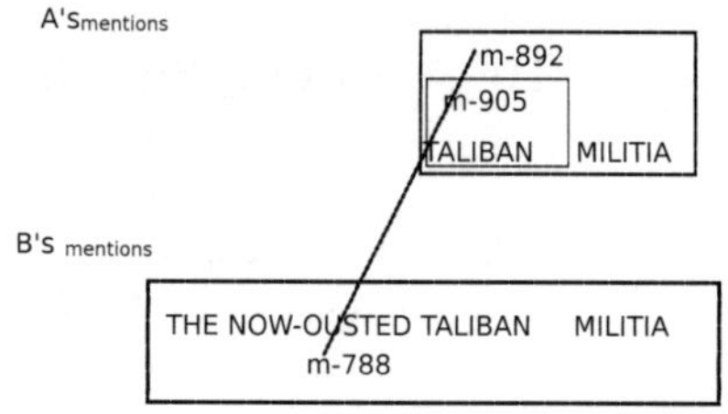

Figure 2: Case of Entity Mention mapping resolved by maximum overlap

2.1 Mapping

As mentioned in the introduction, our system derives a mapping between the entity mentions in Files A and B, as the basis for all further evaluation of the ERE annotations. Entity mentions in Files A and B which have exactly the same location (offset and length) are trivially mapped to each other. We refer to these as "exact" matches.

The remaining cases fall into two categories. One is the case of when an entity mention in one file overlaps with one and only one entity mention in the other file. We refer to these as the "unambiguous" overlapping matches. It is also possible for an entity mention in one file to overlap with more than one entity mention in the other file. We refer to these as the "ambiguous" overlapping matches, and these patterns can get quite complex if multiple ambiguous overlapping matches are involved.

2.1.1 Disambiguation by separate unambiguous mapping

Here an ambiguous overlapping is disambiguated by the presence of an unambiguous mapping, and the choice for mapping the ambiguous case is decided by the desire to maximize the number of mapped entity mentions.

Figure 1 shows such a case. File A has two entity mentions annotations (m-502 and m-463) and File B has two entity mention annotations (m-398 and m-892). These all refer to the same span of text, so m-502 (THE EAST) and m-463 (SOUTH OF IRAN) both overlap with m-398 in File B (THE EAST AND SOUTH OF IRAN). m-463 in addition overlaps with m-892 (IRAN).

We approach the mapping from the perspective of File A. If we assign the mapping for m-463 to be m-398, it will leave m-502 without a match, since m-398 will already be used in the mapping. Therefore, we assign m-502 and m-398 to map to each other, while m-463 and m-892 are mapped to each other. The goal is to match as many mentions as possible, which this accomplishes.

2.1.2 Disambiguation by maximum overlap

The other case is shown in Figure 2. Here there are two mentions in File A, m-892 (TALIBAN MILITIA) and m-905 (TALIBAN), both overlapping with one mention in File B, m-788 (THE NOW-OUSTED TALIBAN MILITIA), so it is not possible to have a matching of all the mentions. We choose the mapping with greatest overlap, in terms of characters, and so m-892 and m-788 are taken to match, while m-905 is left without a match.

For such cases of disambiguation by maximum overlap, it may be possible that a different matching, the one with less overlap, might be a better fit for one of the higher levels of annotation. This issue will be resolved in the future by using ENTITIES rather than ENTITY MENTIONS as the units to compare for the RELATION and EVENT levels.

2.2 Categorization of annotation inconsistencies

Our system produces an entity mention report that lists the number of exact matches, the number of overlap matches, and for Files A and B how many entity mentions each had that did not have a corresponding match in the other annotator's file.

Entity mentions can overlap in different ways, some of which are more "serious" than other. We categorize each overlapping entity mention based on the nature of the edge differences in the non-exact match, such as the presence or absence of a determiner or punctuation, or other material.

In addition, both exact and overlap mentions can match based on location, but be different as far as the entity mention level (NAMed, NOMinal, and PROnominal). The software also outputs all such mismatches for each match.

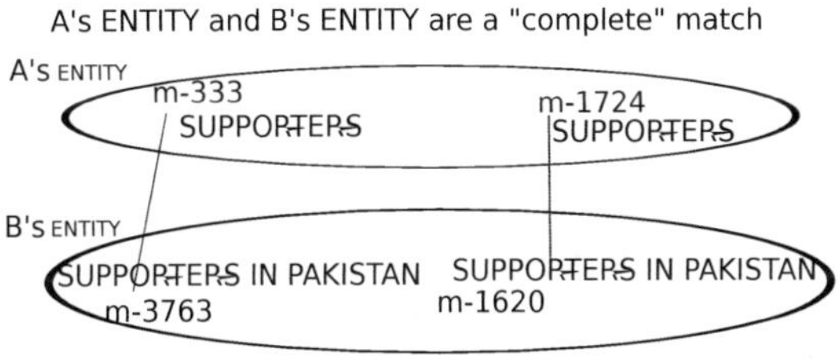

Figure 3: Complete match between File A and File B ENTITIES despite overlapping mentions

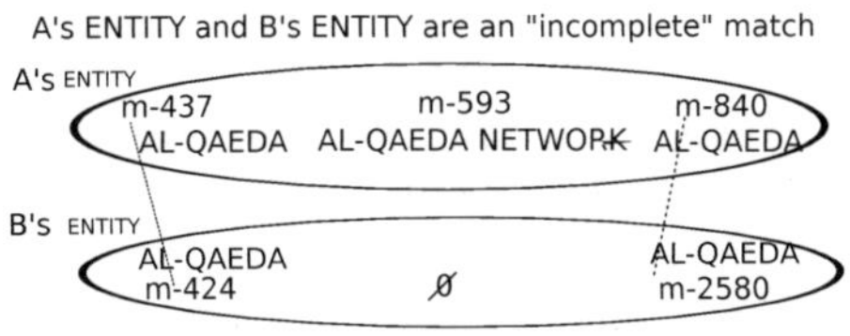

Figure 4: Incomplete match between File A and File B ENTITIES, because File B does not have a mention corresponding to m-593 in File A

3 Entities

An ENTITY is a group of coreferenced entity mentions. We use the entity mention mapping discussed in Section 2 to categorize matches between the ENTITIES as follows:

Complete match: This means that for some ENTITY x in File A and ENTITY y in File B, there is a 1-1 correspondence between the mentions of these two ENTITIES. For purposes of this categorization, we do not distinguish between exact and overlap mapping but include both as corresponding mention instances, because this distinction was already reported as part of the mention mapping.

Figure 3 shows an example of a complete match. File A has two mentions, m-333 (SUPPORTERS) and m-1724 (another instance of SUPPORTERS). These are co-referenced together to form a single ENTITY. In File B there are two mentions, m-3763 (SUPPORTERS IN PAKISTAN) an m-1620 (another instance of SUPPORTERS IN PAKISTAN). It was determined by the algorithm for entity mention mapping in Section 2.1 that m-333 and m-3763 are mapped to each other, as are m-1724 and m-1620, although each pair of mentions is an overlapping match, not an exact match. At the ENTITY level of coferences mentions, there is a 1-1 mapping between the mentions of A's ENTITY and B's ENTITY. Therefore these two ENTITIES are categorized as having a complete mapping between them.

Incomplete match: This means that for some ENTITY x in file A and ENTITY y in file B, there may be some mentions that are part of x in A that have no match in File B, but all the mentions that are part of x map to mentions that are part of ENTITY y in File B, and vice-versa. Figure 4 shows an example of an incomplete match. File A has three entity mentions, m-437 (AL-QAEDA), m-593 (AL-QAEDA NETWORK), and m-840 (AL-QAEDA again), coreferenced together as a single ENTITY. File B has two entity mentions, m-424 (AL-QAEDA) and m-2580 (AL-QAEDA again), coreferenced together as a single ENTITY. While m-437 maps to m-424 and m-840 maps to m-2580, m-593 does not have a match in File B, causing this to be categorized as an incomplete match.

No match: It is possible that some ENTITIES may not map to an ENTITY in the other file, if the conditions for neither type of match exist. For example, if in Figure 4 m-593 mapped to a mention in File B that was part of a different ENTITY than m-424 and m-2580, then there would not be even an incomplete match between the two ENTITIES.

Similar to the mentions, ENTITIES as a whole can match as complete or incomplete, but still differ on the entity type (ORGanization, PERson, etc.). We output such type mismatches as separate information for the ENTITY matching.

4 Relations

A RELATION is defined as having:

1) Two RELATION arguments, each of which is an ENTITY.
2) An optional "trigger", a span of text.
3) A type and subtype. (e.g., "Physical.Located")

For this preliminary stage of the system, we match RELATIONS in a similar way as we do the ENTITIES, by matching the corresponding entity mentions, as stand-ins for the ENTITY arguments for the RELATION. We use the previously-established mapping of mentions as basis of the RELATION mapping.[2]

We report four types of RELATION matching:[3]
1) exact match - This is the same as the complete

[2]This is a stricter mapping requirement than is ultimately necessary, and future work will adjust the basis of RELATION mapping to be full ENTITIES.

[3]Because of space reasons and because RELATIONS are so similar to EVENTS, we do not show here an illustration of RELATION mapping.

match for ENTITIES, except in addition checking for a trigger match and type/subtype.
2) types different - a match for the arguments, although the type or subtypes of the RELATIONS do not match. (The triggers may or may not be different for this case.)
3) triggers different - a match for the arguments and type/subtype, although with different triggers.
4) no match - the arguments for a RELATION in one file do not map to arguments for any one single RELATION in the other file.

5 Events

The structure of an EVENT is similar to that of a RELATION. Its components are:

1) One or more EVENT arguments. Each EVENT argument is an ENTITY or a date.
2) An obligatory trigger argument.
3) A type and subtype (e.g., "Life.MARRY")

In contrast to RELATIONS, the trigger argument is obligatory. There must be at least one ENTITY argument (or a date argument) in order for the EVENT to qualify for annotation, although it does not need to be exactly two, as with RELATIONS.

The mapping between EVENTS works essentially as for ENTITIES and RELATIONS, once again based on the already-established mapping of the entity mentions.[4] There are two slight twists, however. It is possible for the only EVENT argument to be a date, which is not an entity mention, and so we must also establish a mapping for EVENT date arguments, as we did for the entity mentions. Because the trigger is obligatory, we treat it with the same level of importance as the arguments, and establish a mapping between EVENT triggers as well. We report three types of EVENT matching:[5]

1) exact match - all arguments match, as does the trigger, as well as the type/subtype.
2) types different - a match for the arguments and trigger, although the type or subtypes of the EVENTS do not match.
3) no match - either the arguments for a EVENT in one file do not map to arguments for any one single EVENT in the other file, or the triggers do not map.

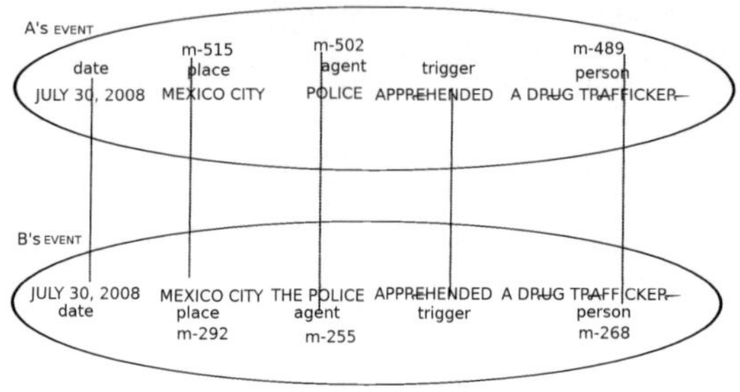

Figure 5: EVENT match

Figure 5 shows an example of an exact match for two EVENTS, one each in File A and B. All of the arguments in one EVENT map to an argument in the other EVENT, as does the trigger. Note that the argument m-502 (an entity mention, POLICE) in File A maps to argument m-255 (an entity mention, THE POLICE) in File B as an overlap match, although the EVENTS are considered an exact match.

6 Future work

We did these comparisons based on the lowest entity mention level in order to develop a preliminary system. However, the arguments for EVENTS and RELATIONS are ENTITIES, not entity mentions, and the system be adjusted to do the correct comparison. Work to adjust the system in this direction is in progress. When the full system is in place in this way, we will report results as well. In future work we will be developing a quantitative scoring metric based on the work described here.

Acknowledgments

This material is based on research sponsored by Air Force Research Laboratory and Defense Advance Research Projects Agency under agreement number FA8750-13-2-0045. The U.S. Government is authorized to reproduce and distribute reprints for Governmental purposes notwithstanding any copyright notation thereon. The views and conclusions contained herein are those of the authors and should not be interpreted as necessarily representing the official policies or endorsements, either expressed or implied, of Air Force Research Laboratory and Defense Advanced Research Projects Agency or the U.S. Government.

[4] As with relations, this is a stricter mapping than necessary, and future work will adjust to use ENTITIES as EVENT arguments.

[5] Currently, if an EVENT argument does not map to any mention in the other file, we consider the EVENT to be a "no match". In the future we will modify this (and likewise for RELATIONS) to be more forgiving, along the lines of the "incomplete match" for ENTITIES.

References

George Doddington, Alexis Mitchell, Mark Przybocki, Lance Ramshaw, Stephanie Strassel, and Ralph Weischedel. 2004. Automatic content extraction (ACE) program - task definitions and performance measures. In *LREC 2004: 4th International Conference on Language Resources and Evaluation*.

Seth Kulick, Ann Bies, Justin Mott, Mohamed Maamouri, Beatrice Santorini, and Anthony Kroch. 2013. Using derivation trees for informative treebank inter-annotator agreement evaluation. In *Proceedings of the 2013 Conference of the North American Chapter of the Association for Computational Linguistics: Human Language Technologies*, pages 550–555, Atlanta, Georgia, June. Association for Computational Linguistics.

LDC. 2014a. DEFT ERE Annotation Guidelines: Entities v1.6. Technical report, Linguistic Data Consortium.

LDC. 2014b. DEFT ERE Annotation Guidelines: Events v1.3. Technical report, Linguistic Data Consortium.

LDC. 2014c. DEFT ERE Annotation Guidelines: Relations v1.3. Technical report, Linguistic Data Consortium.

Unsupervised Techniques for Extracting and Clustering Complex Events in News

Delia Rusu *
Jožef Stefan Institute and
Jožef Stefan International
Postgraduate School
Ljubljana, Slovenia
delia.rusu@ijs.si

James Hodson, Anthony Kimball
Bloomberg Labs
New York, NY, USA
{jhodson2,akimball2}
@bloomberg.net

Abstract

Structured machine-readable representations of news articles can radically change the way we interact with information. One step towards obtaining these representations is event extraction - the identification of event triggers and arguments in text. With previous approaches mainly focusing on classifying events into a small set of predefined types, we analyze unsupervised techniques for complex event extraction. In addition to extracting event mentions in news articles, we aim at obtaining a more general representation by disambiguating to concepts defined in knowledge bases. These concepts are further used as features in a clustering application. Two evaluation settings highlight the advantages and shortcomings of the proposed approach.

1 Introduction

Event extraction is a key prerequisite for generating structured, machine-readable representations of natural language. Such representations can aid various tasks like a) question answering, by enabling systems to provide results for more complex queries, b) machine translation, by enhancing different translation models or c) novelty detection, as a basis for computing geometric distances or distributional similarities. Event extraction primarily requires identifying *what* has occurred and *who* or *what* was involved, as well as the *time interval* of the occurrence. Additional information related to the event mention may include its *location*. Moreover, the event mention can also be labeled as belonging to a certain *event type*. Generally speaking, the goal of event extraction is to identify the *event trigger*, i.e. the words that most clearly define the event, and the *event arguments*. For example, the event mention {*Hurricane Katrina struck the coast of New Orleans in August 2005*} belonging to the *occurrence of natural disasters* type of events includes the location of the disaster - *New Orleans* and the time of occurrence - *August 2005*. The event trigger is the verb *struck* while the other words represent the arguments of this event. The generalized form of the event mention is {*natural disaster occurred at location on date*}. Another similar event mention is {*Hurricane Katrina hit New Orleans*}, having the generalized form {*natural disaster occurred at location*}. Both event mentions can be generalized to {*natural disaster occurred at location*}, with the first event mention providing additional details regarding the date of the occurrence.

Supervised approaches imply classifying extracted event mentions according to predefined event types (Hong et al., 2011; Li et al., 2013). Lexical databases such as FrameNet (Baker et al., 1998), VerbNet (Schuler, 2005) or PropBank (Kingsbury and Palmer, 2002) can serve as training data. However, the coverage of this data is still limited, especially for domain-specific applications, and acquiring more labeled data can be expensive. Unsupervised approaches, on the other hand, are usually used to extract large numbers of untyped events (Fader et al., 2011; Nakashole et al., 2012; Alfonseca et al., 2013; Lewis and Steedman, 2013). Despite the coverage of these techniques, some of the extracted events can suffer from reduced quality in terms of both precision and recall. Distant supervision aims at mitigating the disadvantages of both supervised and unsupervised techniques by leveraging events defined in knowledge bases (Mintz et al., 2009).

In this work we investigate unsupervised techniques for extracting and clustering complex events from news articles. For clustering events we are using their generalized representation ob-

*The work was carried out while the first author was an intern with Bloomberg Labs.

Proceedings of the 2nd Workshop on EVENTS: Definition, Detection, Coreference, and Representation, pages 26–34,
Baltimore, Maryland, USA, June 22-27, 2014.

Event pattern	Explanation	Event mention
$\{entity_1, verb, entity_2\}$	an event having two named entities as arguments; verb modifiers are also included	{**Obama**, apologized for problems with, **ACA** rollout}
$\{sub, verb\}$ $\{sub, verb, obj\}$	a sequence of inter-related events having as arguments a subject and an object	{**Obama**, apologized} {**Obama**, offered, fix}
$\{sub, entity_1, verb, obj, entity_2\}$	an event having a subject, an object and two named entities as arguments	{**Hurricane Katrina**, struck, coast, of **New Orleans**}

Table 1: Examples of extracted events from text, where the event triggers are underlined and named entities are marked in bold.

tained by disambiguating events to concepts defined in knowledge bases. We are primarily looking at Bloomberg news articles which have a particular writing style: complicated sentence structures and numerous dependencies between words. In such cases a first challenge is to correctly identify the event trigger and all event arguments. Moreover, an event is described in news in different ways. Therefore, a second challenge is to capture the relations between event mentions. Thirdly, Bloomberg news mainly focuses on financial news reporting. Lexical databases such as FrameNet are intended for the general domain and do not cover most of the events described in financial news.

2 General Approach

We propose the following pipeline for extracting and clustering complex events from news articles. Firstly, we identify events based on the output of a dependency parser. Parsers can capture dependencies between words belonging to different clauses, enabling the detection of sequences of inter-related events. Section 3 describes two complementary approaches to event extraction which leverage dependencies between verbs and shortest paths between entities. Secondly, we obtain more general representations of the events by annotating them with concepts defined in (multilingual) knowledge bases (see Section 4). We refer to such generalized events as *complex events*. The knowledge base structure allows us to experiment with different levels of generalization. As a final step we apply a data-driven clustering algorithm to group similar generalized events. Clustering can be seen as an alternative to labeling events with predefined event types. Details regarding the clustering approach can be found in Section 5.

3 Event Extraction

Most of the previous unsupervised information extraction techniques have been developed for identifying semantic relations (Fader et al., 2011; Nakashole et al., 2012; Lewis and Steedman, 2013). These approaches extract binary relations following the pattern $\{arg_1, \textit{relation}, arg_2\}$. An example of such a relation is {*EBX Group Co., founder, Eike Batista*}, with the arguments of the *founder* relation being *EBX Group Co.* and *Eike Batista*. Similar to relations, events also have *arguments* such as named entities or time expressions (Li et al., 2013). In addition to the arguments, events are also characterized by the presence of an *event trigger*. In this work we consider *verbs* as event triggers, and identify events following the pattern:

$$\{\textit{verb}, arg_1, arg_2, ..., arg_n\},$$

where $arg_1, arg_2, ..., arg_n$ is the list of event arguments. Aside from *named entities* and *time expressions*, we find additional valid argument candidates to be the *subject* or *object* of the clause. Together with the verb we also include its modifiers. Table 1 lists a few examples of extracted events.

In order to extract the events, we use the output of a dependency parser. Dependency parsing has been widely used for relation and event extraction (Nakashole et al., 2012; Alfonseca et al., 2013; Lewis and Steedman, 2013). There are various publicly-available tools providing dependency parse at the sentence level. We use the output of ZPar (Zhang and Clark, 2011), which implements an incremental parsing process with the de-

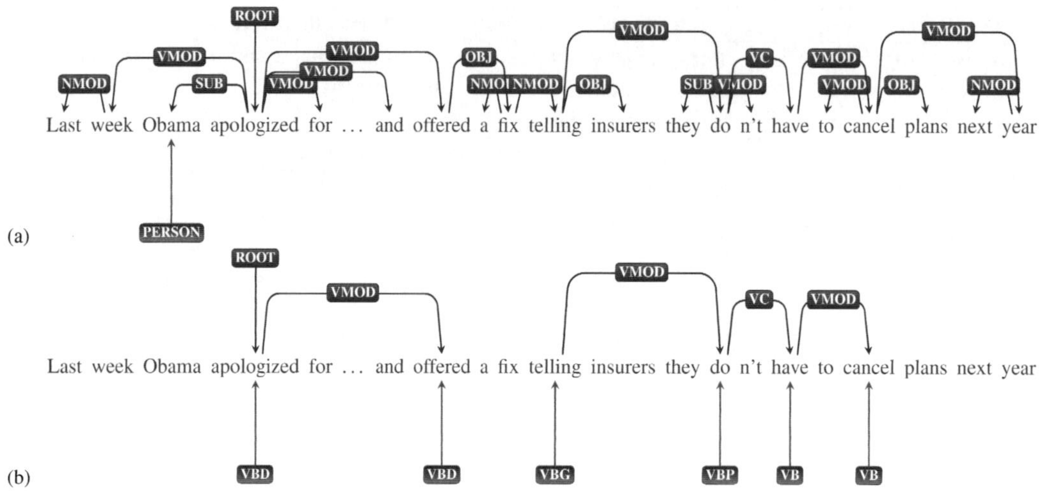

Figure 1: (a) Example sentence with highlighted word dependencies and named entities. (b) Example sentence marked with dependencies between verbs.

coding based on the Beam Search algorithm. The parser processes around 100 sentences per second at above 90% F-score.

The sentences that we are analyzing have a rather complex structure, with numerous dependencies between words. An example sentence is presented in Figure 1 (a). In this example there is a sequence of inter-related events which share the same subject: {*Obama apologized*} and {*Obama offered fix*}. Such events cannot be captured using only simple pattern matching techniques like the one implemented by REVERB (Fader et al., 2011). Other relations that are hard to identify are the lexically distant ones - this is the case with the dependence between the verb *apologized* and the verb *offered*. Consequently, we consider the following two complementary approaches to event extraction, both of them based on the output of the dependency parser:

1. Identifying verbs (including verb modifiers) and their arguments,
2. Identifying shortest paths between entities.

3.1 Identifying Verbs and Their Arguments

In order to identify inter-related events we extract dependency sub-trees for the verbs in the sentence. The verb sub-trees also allow us to extend the argument list with missing arguments. This is the case of the event mention {*Obama offered fix*}, where the subject *Obama* is missing.

The example sentence in Figure 1 (b) contains two verb sub-trees, the first one including the nodes *apologized* and *offered* and the second one including the nodes *telling*, *do*, *have* and *cancel*. Once the sub-trees are identified, we can augment them with their corresponding arguments. For determining the arguments we use the REVERB relation pattern:

$$V|VP|VW^*P,$$

where V matches any verb, VP matches a verb followed by a preposition and VW^*P matches a verb followed by one or more nouns, adjectives, adverbs or pronouns and ending with a preposition.

3.2 Identifying Shortest Paths between Entities

Manual qualitative analysis of the events extracted using the approach described in Subsection 3.1 suggests that the *verbs and arguments* patterns do not cover all the events that are of interest to us. This is the case of events where two or more named entities are involved. For example, for the sentence in Figure 1 (a) we identify the event mentions {*Obama apologized*} and {*Obama offered fix*} using verb and argument patterns, but we cannot identify the event mention {*Obama apologized for problems with ACA rollout*} which includes two named entities: *Obama* and *ACA (Affordable Healthcare Act)*. We therefore expand our set of extracted events by identifying the shortest path connecting all identified entities. This is similar to the work of Bunescu and Mooney (2005) which

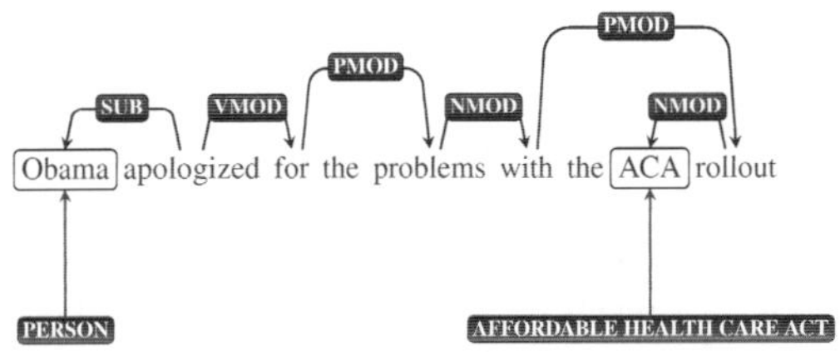

Figure 2: An event mention {*Obama apologized for problems with ACA rollout*} identified using the shortest path between entities approach.

build shortest path dependency kernels for relation extraction, where the shortest path connects two named entities in text.

We first use the Stanford Named Entity Recognizer (Finkel et al., 2005) to detect named entities and temporal expressions in the sentence. Next, we determine the shortest path in the dependency tree linking these entities. An example entity pattern discovered using this approach is shown in Figure 2.

4 Event Disambiguation

We disambiguate the events by annotating each word with WordNet (Fellbaum, 2005) super-senses and BabelNet (Navigli and Ponzetto, 2012) senses and hypernyms. WordNet super-senses offer the highest level of generalization for events, followed by BabelNet hypernyms and BabelNet senses. The choice of annotating with WordNet concepts is motivated by its wide usage as a knowledge base covering the common English vocabulary. There are 41 WordNet super-sense classes defined for nouns and verbs. Table 2 depicts example WordNet super-senses with a short description.

Previous work on annotating text with WordNet super-senses mainly used supervised techniques. Ciaramita and Altun (2006) propose a sequential labeling approach and train a discriminative Hidden Markov Model. Lacking labeled data we investigate simple unsupervised techniques. Firstly, we take into account the first sense heuristic which chooses, from all the possible senses for a given word, the sense which is most frequent in a given corpus. The first sense heuristic has been used as a baseline in many evaluation settings, and it is hard to overcome for unsupervised disambiguation algorithms (Navigli, 2009). Secondly, we use a kernel to compute the similarity between the sentence and the super-sense definition. If x and y are row vectors representing normalized counts of the words in the sentence and the words in the super-sense definition, respectively, the kernel is defined as:

Super-sense	**Description**
communication.noun	communicative processes and contents
quantity.noun	quantities and units of measure
possession.noun	possession and transfer of possession
possession.verb	buying, selling, owning
motion.verb	walking, flying, swimming
stative.verb	being, having, spatial relations

Table 2: Example noun and verb super-sense labels and descriptions taken from WordNet.

$$k(x, y) = \frac{xy^T}{\|x\| \, \|y\|}$$

BabelNet is a multilingual knowledge base, mainly integrating concepts from WordNet and Wikipedia. The current version 2.0 contains 50 languages. We use the BabelNet 1.0.1 knowledge base and API to disambiguate words. As a starting point we consider the PageRank-based disambiguation algorithm provided by the API, but future work should investigate other graph-based algorithms.

5 Event Clustering

Events are clustered based on the features they have in common. We aim at obtaining clusters for the two types of extracted events: verbs and their arguments and shortest paths between entities in the dependency tree. The following two event patterns are considered for this experiment, for both event patterns: {*sub, verb, obj*} and {*sub, verb, obj, entities*}, where the verb and arguments can appear in the sentence in any order. Each event is described using a set of features. These features are extracted for the arguments of each event: the *sub*, *obj* and *entities*. The following feature combinations are used for each argument in the event argument list:

- WordNet super-senses,
- BabelNet senses,

- BabelNet hypernyms,
- WordNet super-senses, BabelNet senses and hypernyms.

For the WordNet experiments we include both disambiguation techniques - using the first sense heuristic and the kernel for determining the similarity between the sentence and the super-sense definition. Similar to the WordNet disambiguation approach we generate vectors for each event, where a vector x includes normalized counts of the argument features for the specific event. Thus we can determine the similarity between two events using the kernel defined in Section 4.

The Chinese Whispers algorithm (Biemann, 2006) presented in Algorithm 1 is used to cluster the events. We opted for this graph-clustering algorithm due to the fact that it is scalable and non-parametric. The highest rank class in the neighborhood of a given event e_i is the class of the event most similar to e_i.

Data: set of events E
Result: class labels for events in E

```
for e_i ∈ E do class(e_i) = i;
while not converged do
    randomize order of events in E;
    for e_i ∈ E do
        class(e_i) = highest ranked class in
        the neighborhood of e_i;
    end
end
```

Algorithm 1: Chinese Whispers Algorithm.

6 Evaluation

We evaluated the extracted events, as well as the clusters obtained for the disambiguated events. For each set of experiments we prepared a dataset by sampling Bloomberg news articles.

As there is no benchmark dataset for the news articles that we are analyzing, we propose to evaluate event extraction in terms of completeness. Clustering evaluation is done based on the model itself, and for different feature combinations. In what follows we describe the evaluation setting in more detail.

6.1 Event Extraction Evaluation

The evaluation dataset consists of a sample of 23 stories belonging to the *MEDICARE* topic, containing a total of 1088 sentences. The event extraction algorithms yields 229 entity paths and 515 verb and argument events. Each event is assessed in terms of completeness; an event is deemed to be *complete* if all event elements (the event trigger and the arguments) are correctly identified. We only analyze two event patterns: $\{$*sub, verb, obj*$\}$ and $\{$*sub, verb, obj, entities*$\}$, as events belonging to other patterns are rather noisy. Two annotators independently rate each event with 1 if all event elements are correctly identified, and 0 otherwise. Note that incomplete events receive a 0 score. Cohen's kappa coefficient (Cohen, 1960) of inter-annotator agreement for this experiment was 0.70. The entity path approach correctly identified 78.6% of the entities while the verb arguments approach identified 69.1% of the events. Events obtained using entity paths tend to have a higher number of arguments compared to the verb arguments approach; this explains the higher score obtained by this technique.

6.2 Clustering Evaluation

As we do not know the cluster labels a priori, we opt for evaluating the clusters using the model itself. To this end, we use the *Silhouette Coefficient* (Kaufman and Rousseeuw, 1990); we plan to investigate other clustering evaluation metrics in future work. The Silhouette Coefficient is defined for each sample, and it incorporates two scores:

$$s = \frac{b - a}{max(a, b)},$$

where a is the mean distance between a sample and all other points within the same class whereas b is the mean distance to all other points in the next nearest class. To determine the coefficient for a set of samples one needs to find the mean of the coefficient for each sample. A higher coefficient score is associated with a model having better defined clusters. The best clustering model will obtain a Silhouette coefficient of 1, while the worst one will obtain a -1 score. Values close to 0 imply overlapping clusters. Negative values signify that the model assigned samples to the wrong cluster, as a different cluster is more similar.

The evaluation dataset comprises 325 *MEDICARE* news articles and 16,450 sentences. In this dataset we identify 7,491 verb and argument events and 2,046 shortest path events. Table 3 shows example events belonging to two event

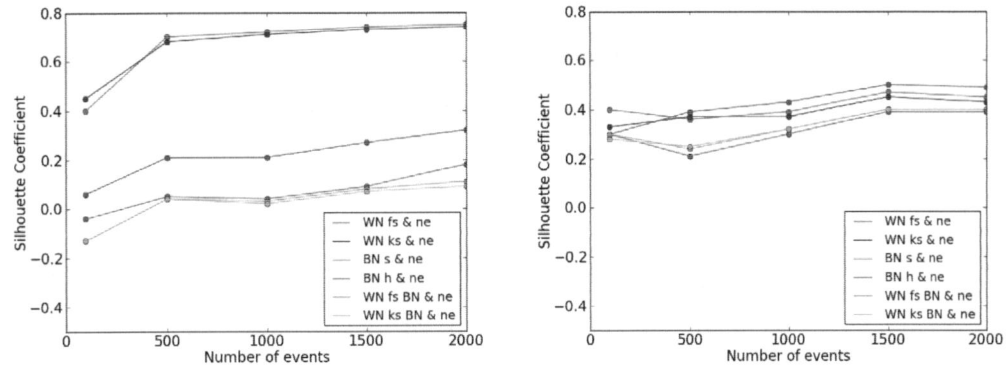

Figure 3: Clustering evaluation results for verbs and arguments (left) and shortest paths between entities (right) events, using different feature combinations.

clusters. The first cluster is obtained by extracting verb argument events while the second cluster is composed of shortest entity path events.

In Figure 3 we show clustering evaluation results for the (a) verbs and arguments and (b) shortest paths between entities, using different feature combinations. As expected, the best results are obtained in the case of the WordNet super-senses, which are the most generic senses assigned to the events. There is less overlap among the BabelNet senses and hypernyms, although results improve as more data is available. The results also mark the difference between the two types of events: verbs and arguments versus shortest paths between entities. Events extracted using the entity path approach tend to have a higher number of arguments, which in turn implies a richer set of features. This explains the higher scores obtained in the case of shortest path events compared to verb argument events.

7 Related Work

The event extraction task have received a lot of attention in recent years, and numerous approaches, both supervised and unsupervised, have been proposed. This section attempts to summarize the main findings.

Supervised approaches. These approaches classify events based on a number of predefined event types. A popular dataset is the NIST Automatic Content Extraction (ACE) corpora (Doddington et al., 2004) which consists of labeled relations and events in text. State-of-the-art approaches mainly use sequential pipelines to separately identify the event trigger and the arguments (Hong et al., 2011). More recently Li et al. (2013) propose a joint framework which considers event triggers and arguments together. Their model is based on structured perceptron with Beam Search. In another line of work (Alfonseca et al., 2013) events extracted in an unsupervised manner from the output of a dependency parser are the building blocks of a Noisy-OR model for headline generation. Tannier and Moriceau (2013) identify event threads in news, i.e. a succession of events in a story, using a cascade of classifiers.

Mintz et al. (2009) propose a distant supervision approach. They use Freebase relations and find sentences which contain entities appearing in these relations. From the sentences the authors extract a number of textual features which are used for relation classification. Dependency parsing features are used to identify relations that are lexically distant.

Unsupervised approaches. Most unsupervised approaches have been tailored to identifying relations in text. Fader et al. (2011) extract relations and their arguments based on part-of-speech patterns. However, such patterns fail to detect lexically distant relations between words. Therefore, most state-of-the-art unsupervised approaches also rely on sentence parsing. For example, Lewis and Steedman (2013) extract cross-lingual semantic relations from the English and French parses of sentences. Relational patterns extracted from the sentence parse tree have also been generalized to syntactic-ontologic-lexical patterns using a frequent itemset mining approach (Nakashole et al., 2012). Poon and Domingos (2009)

Event	Features
{owners are being incentivized to drop their health insurance coverage} {analysts are not permitted receive compensation directly}	noun.person noun.possession noun.person noun.possession
{HHS General issued report in July 2013} {lawmakers asked Kathleen Sebelius to respond by December 6}	noun.person noun.group noun.time noun.person noun.time

Table 3: Example events belonging to two event clusters. Each event is assigned WordNet supersense features.

learn a semantic parser using Markov logic by converting dependency trees into quasi-logical forms which are clustered.

DIRT (Lin and Pantel, 2001) is an unsupervised method for discovering inference rules from text. The authors leverage the dependency parse of a sentence in order to extract indirect semantic relations of the form "X $relation$ Y" between two words X and Y. Inference rules such as "X $relation_1$ $Y \approx X$ $relation_2$ Y" are determined based on the similarity of the relations.

ALICE (Banko and Etzioni, 2007) is a system that iteratively discovers concepts, relations and their generalizations from the Web. The system uses a data-driven approach to expand the core concepts defined by the WordNet lexical database with instances from its Web corpus. These instances are identified by applying predefined extraction patterns. The relations extracted using TextRunner (Banko et al., 2007) are generalized using a clustering-based approach.

Our aim is to identify events rather than any relation between two concepts. We therefore propose different extraction patterns based on the dependency parse of a sentence which allow us to detect event triggers and event arguments that can be lexically distant. Events are generalized by mapping them to concepts from two different knowledge bases (WordNet and BabelNet), allowing us to experiment with multiple levels of generalization.

8 Conclusions and Future Work

In this work we investigated different unsupervised techniques for extracting and clustering complex events from news articles. As a first step we proposed two complementary event extraction algorithms, based on identifying verbs and their arguments and shortest paths between entities, respectively. Next, we obtained more general representations of the event mentions by annotating the event trigger and arguments with concepts from knowledge bases. The generalized arguments were used as features for a clustering approach, thus determining related events.

As future work on the event extraction side, we plan to improve event quality by learning a model for filtering out noisy events. In the case of event disambiguation we are looking into different graph-based disambiguation algorithms to enhance concept annotations.

Acknowledgments

We would like to thank Pierre Brunelle and Konstantine Arkoudas as well as the anonymous reviewers for their helpful comments. This work was funded by Bloomberg LP and the ICT Programme of the EC under XLike (ICT-STREP-288342).

References

[Alfonseca et al.2013] Enrique Alfonseca, Daniele Pighin, and Guillermo Garrido. 2013. Heady: News headline abstraction through event pattern clustering. In *Proceedings of the 51st Annual Meeting of the Association for Computational Linguistics*, pages 1243–1253.

[Baker et al.1998] Collin F Baker, Charles J Fillmore, and John B Lowe. 1998. The Berkeley Framenet Project. In *Proceedings of the 36th Annual Meeting of the Association for Computational Linguistics and 17th International Conference on Computational Linguistics-Volume 1*, pages 86–90. Association for Computational Linguistics.

[Banko and Etzioni2007] Michele Banko and Oren Etzioni. 2007. Strategies for lifelong knowledge extraction from the web. In *Proceedings of the 4th international conference on Knowledge capture*, pages 95–102. ACM.

[Banko et al.2007] Michele Banko, Michael J Cafarella, Stephen Soderland, Matthew Broadhead, and Oren Etzioni. 2007. Open information extraction for the web. In *IJCAI*, volume 7, pages 2670–2676.

[Biemann2006] Chris Biemann. 2006. Chinese whispers: an efficient graph clustering algorithm and its application to natural language processing problems. In *Proceedings of the first workshop on graph based methods for natural language processing*, pages 73–80. Association for Computational Linguistics.

[Bunescu and Mooney2005] Razvan C Bunescu and Raymond J Mooney. 2005. A shortest path dependency kernel for relation extraction. In *Proceedings of the conference on Human Language Technology and Empirical Methods in Natural Language Processing*, pages 724–731. Association for Computational Linguistics.

[Ciaramita and Altun2006] Massimiliano Ciaramita and Yasemin Altun. 2006. Broad-coverage sense disambiguation and information extraction with a supersense sequence tagger. In *Proceedings of the 2006 Conference on Empirical Methods in Natural Language Processing*, pages 594–602. Association for Computational Linguistics.

[Cohen1960] Jacob Cohen. 1960. A coefficient of agreement for nominal scales. *Educational and Psychological Measurement*, 20(1):37–46.

[Doddington et al.2004] George R Doddington, Alexis Mitchell, Mark A Przybocki, Lance A Ramshaw, Stephanie Strassel, and Ralph M Weischedel. 2004. The automatic content extraction (ace) program-tasks, data, and evaluation. In *LREC*.

[Fader et al.2011] Anthony Fader, Stephen Soderland, and Oren Etzioni. 2011. Identifying relations for open information extraction. In *Proceedings of the Conference on Empirical Methods in Natural Language Processing*, pages 1535–1545. Association for Computational Linguistics.

[Fellbaum2005] Christiane Fellbaum. 2005. Wordnet and wordnets. In Keith et al. Brown, editor, *Encyclopedia of Language and Linguistics*, pages 665–670. Oxford: Elsevier, second edition.

[Finkel et al.2005] Jenny Rose Finkel, Trond Grenager, and Christopher Manning. 2005. Incorporating non-local information into information extraction systems by gibbs sampling. In *Proceedings of the 43rd Annual Meeting on Association for Computational Linguistics*, pages 363–370. Association for Computational Linguistics.

[Hong et al.2011] Yu Hong, Jianfeng Zhang, Bin Ma, Jianmin Yao, Guodong Zhou, and Qiaoming Zhu. 2011. Using cross-entity inference to improve event extraction. In *Proceedings of the 49th Annual Meeting of the Association for Computational Linguistics: Human Language Technologies-Volume 1*, pages 1127–1136. Association for Computational Linguistics.

[Kaufman and Rousseeuw1990] Leonard Kaufman and Peter J Rousseeuw. 1990. *Finding groups in data: an introduction to cluster analysis*. John Wiley & Sons.

[Kingsbury and Palmer2002] Paul Kingsbury and Martha Palmer. 2002. From treebank to propbank. In *Proceedings of the International Conference on Language Resources and Evaluation LREC*.

[Lewis and Steedman2013] Mike Lewis and Mark Steedman. 2013. Unsupervised induction of cross-lingual semantic relations. In *Proceedings of the 2013 Conference on Empirical Methods in Natural Language Processing EMNLP*, pages 681–692.

[Li et al.2013] Qi Li, Heng Ji, and Liang Huang. 2013. Joint event extraction via structured prediction with global features. In *Proceedings of the 51st Annual Meeting of the Association for Computational Linguistics*.

[Lin and Pantel2001] Dekang Lin and Patrick Pantel. 2001. Dirt - discovery of inference rules from text. In *Proceedings of the seventh ACM SIGKDD international conference on Knowledge discovery and data mining*, pages 323–328. ACM.

[Mintz et al.2009] Mike Mintz, Steven Bills, Rion Snow, and Dan Jurafsky. 2009. Distant supervision for relation extraction without labeled data. In *Proceedings of the Joint Conference of the 47th Annual Meeting of the ACL and the 4th International Joint Conference on Natural Language Processing of the AFNLP: Volume 2*, pages 1003–1011. Association for Computational Linguistics.

[Nakashole et al.2012] Ndapandula Nakashole, Gerhard Weikum, and Fabian Suchanek. 2012. Patty: a taxonomy of relational patterns with semantic types. In *Proceedings of the 2012 Joint Conference on Empirical Methods in Natural Language Processing and Computational Natural Language Learning*, pages 1135–1145. Association for Computational Linguistics.

[Navigli and Ponzetto2012] Roberto Navigli and Simone Paolo Ponzetto. 2012. Babelnet: The automatic construction, evaluation and application of a wide-coverage multilingual semantic network. *Artificial Intelligence*, 193:217–250.

[Navigli2009] Roberto Navigli. 2009. Word sense disambiguation: A survey. *ACM Computing Surveys (CSUR)*, 41(2):10.

[Poon and Domingos2009] Hoifung Poon and Pedro Domingos. 2009. Unsupervised semantic parsing. In *Proceedings of the 2009 Conference on Empirical Methods in Natural Language Processing: Volume 1-Volume 1*, pages 1–10. Association for Computational Linguistics.

[Schuler2005] Karin Kipper Schuler. 2005. Verbnet: A broad-coverage, comprehensive verb lexicon.

[Tannier and Moriceau2013] Xavier Tannier and Véronique Moriceau. 2013. Building event threads out of multiple news articles. Proceedings of the 2013 Conference on Empirical Methods in Natural Language Processing EMNLP.

[Zhang and Clark2011] Yue Zhang and Stephen Clark. 2011. Syntactic processing using the generalized perceptron and beam search. *Computational Linguistics*, 37(1):105–151.

Conceptual and Practical Steps in Event Coreference Analysis of Large-scale Data

Fatemeh Torabi Asr[1], Jonathan Sonntag[2], Yulia Grishina[2] and Manfred Stede[2]
[1]MMCI Cluster of Excellence, Saarland University, Germany
fatemeh@coli.uni-saarland.de
[2]Applied Computational Linguistics, University of Potsdam, Germany
sonntag|grishina|stede@uni-potsdam.de

Abstract

A simple conceptual model is employed to investigate events, and break the task of coreference resolution into two steps: semantic class detection and similarity-based matching. With this perspective an algorithm is implemented to cluster event mentions in a large-scale corpus. Results on test data from AQUAINT TimeML, which we annotated manually with coreference links, reveal how semantic conventions vs. information available in the context of event mentions affect decisions in coreference analysis.

1 Introduction

In a joint project with political scientists, we are concerned with various tasks of indexing the content of a large corpus of newspaper articles. To supplement other NLP tools and as an interesting information for the political scientists by itself, we are interested in keeping track of discussions around headline events such as attacks and crises. The main challenges in the project include:

1. proposing a definition of event identity, and

2. finding the actual mentions in natural text,

to construct clusters of, so-called, coreferential events. We refer to the former task as a *formal convention*, a vital step in order for useful results to be delivered to the human text analysts. The latter is basically an information extraction task once a clear problem specification is obtained.

The main objective of the paper is to shed light on each of the above tasks by applying a three-layer event ontology[1]. Terminologies from earlier theories (Davidson, 1969) up until recent work (Hovy et al., 2013a) are combined to draw an integrated picture of the event coreference problem. The semantic layer is established with the help of WordNet synsets. Related entities and timestamps are considered as fundamental event attributes that in practice can be resolved from the context of a mention. We implement an incremental event clustering algorithm with respect to the adapted ontology of events and use a minimal linguistic procedure to extract values from text for every event attribute. This system is being developed to work within a pipeline annotation project where incremental clustering performs efficiently on large-scale data.

In order to evaluate our proposed method, we have manually annotated a random selection of event mentions in the AQUAINT TimeML corpus (UzZaman et al., 2013). Performance of the automatic system in pair-wise coreference resolution is comparable to that of more sophisticated clustering methods, which at the same time consider a variety of linguistic features (Bejan and Harabagiu, 2010). The differences between the human annotator pair-wise decisions and the output of our clustering algorithm reveal interesting cases where coreference labeling is performed based upon the adapted semantic convention rather than information available in the text about time, location and participants of an event instance. In the following, we provide an overview of the adapted ontology, background on event coreference, and finally our implementation and experiments within the proposed framework on real data as well as the annotated corpus. We point to related work at the various appropriate places in the paper.

2 An Object Oriented Ontology

The general impression one gets by a review of the coreference literature, is that at the semantic

[1]The term ontology is used to refer to a conceptual model of events and connections between them rather than a particular knowledge base implementation.

Proceedings of the 2nd Workshop on EVENTS: Definition, Detection, Coreference, and Representation, pages 35–44,
Baltimore, Maryland, USA, June 22-27, 2014.

formalism level, events are engaged with a higher degree of complexity and more variety than entities. That is probably because of the concrete nature of entities: intuitively, an event *happens*, whereas, an entity *exists*. As a subject matter, the latter is more straightforward to get decomposed into smaller components and be identified by certain feature attributes. The ontology explained in this chapter is general in the sense that one could (perhaps should) start understanding it by examples about entities.

A realized entity belongs to a class of entities sharing the same set of attributes. For example, president Obama, as long as being talked in a political context is considered as an instance of the class `PRESIDENT`, comprising attributes such as `Country`, `Party` and `Duration` of presidency. Any other president can be compared against Obama, with respect to the attribute values associated with them. Therefore, Bush is a different instance of the class `PRESIDENT` regarding the fact that a different political `Party` as well as a different presidential `Duration` are assigned to him. Detecting mentions of these `PRESIDENT` instances in text corpora would be a technical task once the semantic representation was fixed. At this level, instead we face questions like, whether or not a named entity somewhere in the text detected by our text processor, e.g., "Barack Hossein", is referring to the one `PRESIDENT` instance that we named above as Obama.

Figure 1 illustrates similar levels of abstraction for event classes, event instances, and event mentions. The distinction between the second and the third layer are more obvious and previously considered as clearly in other frameworks. The distinction between the first and the second layer, though, is often left implicit, even in recently published event annotation guidelines. For example in a *Grounded Annotation for Events* (GAF, Fokkens et al. 2013), event mentions are clearly distinguished from instances. However, the first two layers have been taken as one, i.e., the *semantic layer*. In their work, *event type* which is an artifact of the adapted semantic ontology (SEM, Klyne and Carroll 2004), implicitly works similar to the classes in our definition. Nevertheless, these three layers are intuitively separable and familiar for linguists working on event and entity recognition. Bejan and Harabagiu (2010), for example, introduce the event coreference resolution with an example put into a similar three-layer hierarchy, despite their purely data-driven approach leaving off prior semantic specifications. Here, we explain each layer of the model separately. Issues specific to coreference detection will be presented in the following section.

2.1 Event Classes

The first layer of the ontology determines event type definitions. Each class can have totally different attributes depending on the interests of a particular study. Some events might be identified only by their time and place, while others by participants of prioritized importance. A very flat semantic representation would attribute all types of events with a fixed set of entities, e.g.: participants, time and location. Note, however, that structural and semantic differences exist among events of different natures, even if these complex phenomena are reduced into something more familiar and tangible such as verb frames (Fillmore et al., 2003). For example, a `KILLING` event is essentially attributed with its `Agent` and `Patient`, while salient attributes of an `EARTHQUAKE` include `Location`, `Magnitude`, `Time` and `Human Impacts`, in a typical news context. This becomes even more clear when event types are taken and compared against one another from different genres of text (Pivovarova et al., 2013; Shaw, 2013). A scientific attitude toward the analysis of `EARTHQUAKE` events might characterize them with `Natural Impacts` rather than `Human Impacts`. Thus, the first layer of the model needs to be designed with respect to the specific information extraction goals of the particular study, be it a pure linguistic or an application-oriented one.

Ambiguities about the granularity of attributes, subevent-ness, scope and most importantly, identity between event instances are dealt with at the definition layer for and between classes. For example, if the modeler wants to allow coreference between instances of `KILLING` and `SHOOTING` to indicate some type of coreference between an event and its possible subevent then this needs to be introduced at the class level, along with a procedure to compare instances of the two classes, which possess different sets of attribute[2]. Remarks

[2]The same applies even to a more flexible case, when the modeler wants to allow coreference between `KILLING` and `DYING` instances (e.g., if a `KILLING`'s `Patient` is the same as a `DYING`'s `Theme`).

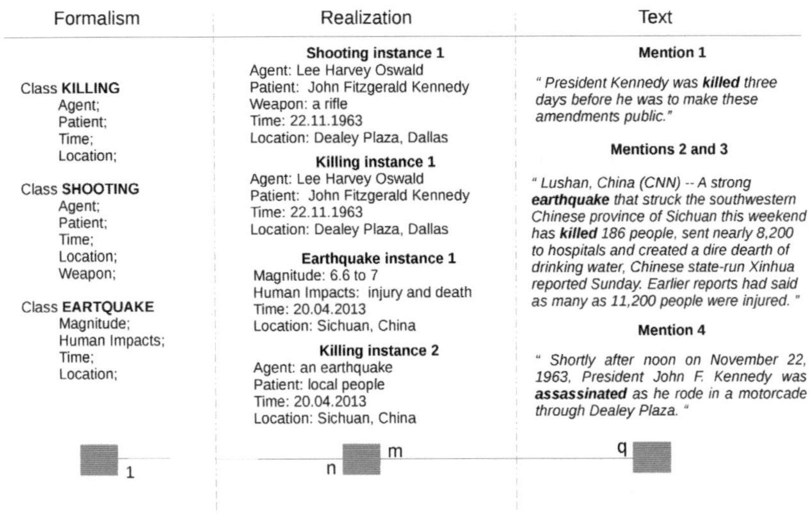

Figure 1: A three-layer ontology of events: classes, instances and mentions

of Hovy et al. (2013b) on different types of identity according to lexicosyntactic similarity, synonymy and paraphrasing indicate that the modelers have a wide choice of identity definition for event types. In section 4.3 we explain how to adapt an extended version of synonymy in order to define event classes prior to similarity-based clustering of the mentions.

2.2 Event Instances

Layer 2 indicates perfect instantiation, representative of the human common sense intuition of phenomena in real world. Instances in this layer correspond to the Davidsonian notion of events as concrete objects with certain locations in space-time, something that is happening, happened, or will happen at some point (Davidson, 1969). Therefore, links from classes to instances represent a one-to-many relation. Every instance of the `EARTHQUAKE` is determined with a unique set of attribute values. Two `EARTHQUAKE` instantiations with exactly similar attribute values are just identical. In order to keep a clear and simple representation specific to the study of coreference, the model does not allow any connection or relation between two event instances unless via their classes. Note that in Figure 1, for each realized object, only attributes included in the formalism layer are presented with their values, while in reality events occur with possibly infinite number of attributes.

2.3 Event Mentions

Facing an event mention in the text, one should first determine its class and then the unique event instance, to which the mention points. Detection of the class depends on the semantic layer definitions, while discovering the particular instance that the mention is talking about relies on the attribute values extractable from the mention context.

Usually, mentions provide only partial information about their target event instance. They can be compared against one another and (if available) against a fully representative mention, which most clearly expresses the target event by providing all necessary attribute values. Fokkens et al. (2013) refer to such a mention as the *trigger event*. Sometimes it is possible that the context is even more informative than necessary to resolve the unique real world corresponding event (see details about the impact of the earthquake in mention 3, Figure 1). In natural text a mention can refer to more than one event instance of the same type, for example when a plural case is used: " ... *droughts, floods and earthquakes cost China 421 billion yuan in 2013*". Hovy et al. (2013b) propose partial coreference between singular and plural mentions. In our model plural mentions are not treated semantically differently, they only point to several instances, thus, are coreferential with any single mention of them as long as the attribute values allow[3].

With respect to the above discussion, links from layer 2 to 3 represent many-to-many relations: an event instance can have several mentions in the text, and a single mention can point to more than one event instance at a time.

3 Towards Coreference Analysis

In terms of method, two different approaches have been tried in the literature under the notion of event coreference resolution (Chen and Ji, 2009; Bejan and Harabagiu, 2010; Lee et al., 2012; Hovy et al., 2013b). The first and most theoretically founded strategy is to decide for every pair of event mentions, whether or not they refer to the same event instance. Since in this approach decisions are independently made for every pair of event mentions, a clear formalism is needed to determine exactly what types of coreference are possible and how they are detected by looking at textual mentions (Chen and Ji, 2009; Hovy et al., 2013b). Some related work on predicate alignment also fit into this category of research (Roth and Frank, 2012; Wolfe et al., 2013). Alternatively, in automatic event clustering, the objective is basically discovering event instances: all we know about an event in the world is the collective information obtained from mentions referring to that in a text corpus. Each cluster in the end ideally represents a unique event in reality with all its attribute values (Bejan and Harabagiu, 2010; Lee et al., 2012). Some formal and technical differences exist between the two approaches.

Boolean choice: traditionally, clusters shape with the idea that all mentions within a cluster are of the same identity. Every randomly chosen pair of mentions are coreferent if they are found in a single cluster at the end, and non-coreferent otherwise. Therefore, taking this approach implies a level of formalism, which rules out partial coreference. On the other hand, pair-wise classification could consider partial coreference whenever two event mentions are neither identical nor totally different (Hovy et al., 2013b). Soft-clustering can compensate some deficiencies of traditional clustering approaches[4].

Transitivity: all mentions in a single cluster are coreferential, whereas pair-wise labels allow for non-transitive relations among event mentions. Depending on the specific goal of a study, this could be an advantage or a disadvantage. Lack of transitivity could be considered as an error if it is not consciously permitted in the underlying semantic formalism.

Complexity and coverage: event mentions can appear in noisy or sparse context where information for detection of their target event instance is not available. Dealing with such cases is usually easier in a clustering framework where similarity scores are calculated against the collective information obtained from a population of mentions, rather than an individual occurrence. Classification approaches could comparatively handle this only if sufficiently representative labeled data is available for training.

Exploration: a general advantage of cluster analysis is that it provides an exploratory framework to assess the nature of similar input records, and at the end it results in a global distributional representation. This is specially desired here, since computational research on event coreference is in its early ages. Evaluation corpora and methodology are still not established, thus, the problem is not yet in the phase of "look for higher precision"!

The method we are going to propose in the next section combines a rule-based initial stage with a similarity-based clustering procedure. This is partially inspired by the work of Rao et al. (2010), where entity coreference links are looked up in high-volume streaming data. They employ a lexicon of named entities for cluster nomination to reduce the search space. Once a mention is visited only the candidates among all incrementally constructed clusters up to that point are examined. Incremental clustering strategies are in general suitable for a pipeline project by efficiently providing single visits of every mention in its context. Feature values of a mention can be extracted from the document text, used for clustering, and combined

[3]The other type of quasi-identity discussed by Hovy et al. (2013b) engaged with sub-events is handled in the semantic level.

[4]For example, multi-assignment would allow plural mentions to take part in several different clusters, each representative of one event instance.

into the feature representation of the assigned cluster in a compressed format.

4 Event Coreference System

The original data in our study is a text corpus automatically annotated with several layers of syntactic and semantic information (Blessing et al., 2013). The English portion includes news and commentary articles of several British and American publishers from 1990 to 2012. An approximate average of 100 event mentions per document with the large number of total documents per month (avg. 1200) requires us to think of different ways to reduce the search space and also design a low-complexity coreference resolution algorithm.

4.1 Partitioning

In cross-document analysis, typically, a topic-based document partitioning is performed prior to the coreference chain detection (Lee et al., 2012; Cybulska and Vossen, 2013). Since we are interested to track discussions about a certain event possibly appearing in different contexts, this technique is not desired as coreference between mentions of a single real word event in two different topics would remain unknown. For example, when an articles reviews several instances of a certain event type such as different attacks that has happened in a wide temporal range and in different locations, such articles would not be included in any of the individual topics each focused on one event instance. As an alternative to the previous approach, we perform a time-window partitioning based on the article publication date before feeding the data into the coreference analysis algorithm. Larger windows would capture more coreference links: this is a parameter that can be set with respect to the available resources in trade-off with the desired search scope. In the future, we would like to invent an efficient procedure to combine the resulting clusters from consecutive time-windows in order to further enhance the recall of the system.

4.2 Event Mention and Feature Identification

In order to extract event mentions we use the ClearTK UIMA library (Ogren et al., 2008), check the PoS of the head word in the extracted text span and take all verbal and nominal mentions into account. In the current implementation all event classes are identified by a fixed set of attributes including `Timestamps` and `Related Entities`. While being very coarse-grained, this way of attribution is quite intuitive: events are identified by times, places and participants directly or vaguely attached to them. Temporal expressions are extracted also by ClearTK and normalized using SUTime (Chang and Manning, 2012). Named entities of all types except `Date` are used which are obtained from previous work on the same dataset (Blessing et al., 2013).

4.3 The Two-step Algorithm

Having all required annotations, we select a time window and perform the following two steps for event mentions of the TimeML classes `Occurrence`, `I-Action`, `Perception` and `Aspectual`[5].

1) Semantic class identification: WordNet synsets provide a rich resource in order to be adapted as event classes (Fellbaum, 1999). They cover a large lexicon and the variety of relational links between words enables us to specify a clear semantic convention for the coreference system. In addition to the mentions coming from the same synset, we allow coreference between events belonging to two different synsets that are directly connected via hypernymy or morphosemantic links. While every WordNet synset comprises words only from a single part of speech, morphosemantic relations allow the model to establish cross-PoS identity among words sharing a stem with the same meaning which is desired here: observe (verb) and observation (noun)[6]. A Java library is employed to access WordNet annotations (Finlayson, 2014).

2) Similarity-based clustering: A mention is compared against previously constructed clusters with respect to the attribute values that are extractable from its context. In order to fill the `Timestamps` attribute we have employed a back-off strategy: first we look at all time expressions in the same paragraph where the event mention appears, if we found enough temporal information, that would suffice. Otherwise, we look into the content of the entire article for temporal expressions. The `Related Entities` at-

[5] Other types, namely, `Report`, `State` and `I-State` events are not interesting for us, therefore such mentions are simply skipped.

[6] When a mention is visited all compatible synsets according to the head lemma are tried because in the current implementation we do not perform word sense disambiguation.

tribute is filled similarly by looking at the named entities in the context of the event mention. The first step is a procedure to candidate clusters containing mentions of related types. If no cluster is a candidate, a singleton cluster is created and its class is added to the index of visited event types (synsets). If candidate clusters already exist, we calculate the feature-based similarity score for each. If the best score is below a threshold a new singleton cluster is created but in this case for the reason that, perhaps, not a new type but a new event instance is visited.

5 Manual Annotation and Evaluation

The Event Coreference Bank, which is the largest available corpus with cross-document coreference labels, supports only a within topic evaluation (ECB, Bejan and Harabagiu 2010). In order to perform a more realistic evaluation of the method presented in this paper, we selected a subset of events from the AQUAINT TimeML corpus and annotated those with coreferentiality. The AQUAINT TimeML data has recently served as one of the benchmarks in the TempEval shared task (UzZaman et al., 2013) and is available for public use[7]. It contains 73 news report documents from four topics, annotated with 4431 event mentions and 652 temporal expressions which make it suitable for our task. Two main differences between our annotation and the ECB data are: 1) event mentions here are selected semi-randomly[8] and across topics rather than topic-based, 2) they are shown pair-wise to the annotator (in order to catch the transitivity patterns after the analysis), whereas, in the ECB, event mentions are clustered. Furthermore, the data already comes with manually assigned mention boundaries, event types, temporal expressions and links between events and temporal expressions, all according to the TimeML standards (Hobbs and Pustejovsky, 2003). These serve exactly as features that our algorithm uses for construction of clusters. We only had to perform named entity recognition automatically to have data ready for evaluation of the model. The manual annotation of 4950 pairs resulting from 100 selected event mentions ($\frac{100!}{2!(100-2)!}$) was done with the help of a simple user interface, which showed each of the two event mentions within its context to the annotator and asked for pushing `yes`, `no` or `next` (undecided) button to proceed to the next pair. After studying the annotation guideline published by Cybulska and Vossen (2014), our expert spent some hours during a week for the job. Decisions made in shorter than 500 ms were revised afterwards. There was one `no` answer which the annotator found unsure after revision, as it resulted in a transitivity violation, but we left it unchanged due to the nature of pair-wise decisions. In the end we came up with a total of 36 `yes`, and 4914 `no` pairs.

6 Experiments

This section provides an insight into how clusters of event mentions are created for a portion of our large news corpus. We also run the algorithm on the manually annotated data to perform an error analysis.

6.1 Construction of Event Clusters

News text from New York Times and Washington Post are combined to demonstrate a showcase of clustering for a time-window of two weeks (250 articles)[9]. Figure 2 shows the creation curve of event classes (type index entries) and event instances (clusters) as the number of the visited mentions increases. Comparison between the number of mentions with that of clusters indicates that a great deal of event instances are mentioned only once in the text. Since, for each mention, all compatible synsets are added to the type index (if not there already) during the early stages of clustering the number of the type index entries is times the number of visited mentions. In the middle to the end phases the type index contains a large collection of event classes, also a decent number of non-singleton clusters (repeatedly mentioned event instances) are created. Statistics of the type of clusters obtained after performing the algorithm on the processed mentions are presented in Table 1. A significant number of non-singleton clusters contain mentions only from a single paragraph or a single article, which is expected given the type

[7] `http://www.cs.york.ac.uk/semeval-2013/task1`

[8] Since the number of coreferential mentions is much smaller than non-coreferent ones, we adapted a heuristic measure to make sure that we will have some similar mentions among the 100 records. Therefore, we would call it a semi-random selection, still different from the fully selective strategy employed for ECB.

[9] This collection is processed within a few minutes on a normal PC by the proposed algorithm starting with zero clusters.

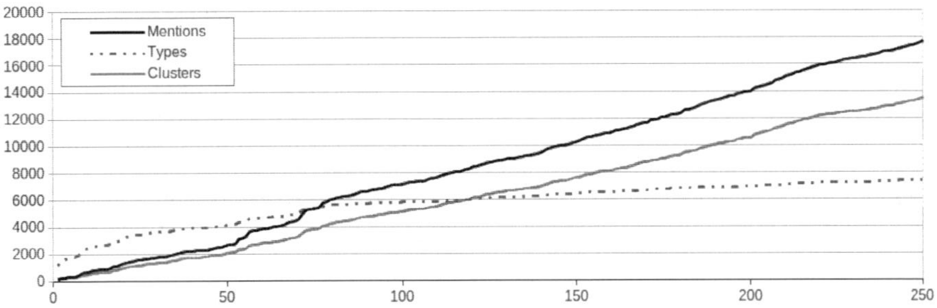

Figure 2: Number of clusters and the type index entries as mentions are visited in 250 articles

of features; remember that `Timestamps` and `Named Entities` are looked up in a paragraph scope. Clusters containing mentions from several articles, namely, the *popular* ones are most interesting for us as they would be representative of the systems performance on cross-document coreference analysis. By looking at those we found that the named entities have a very important role in finding similar subtopics within and between documents. Temporal expressions are less helpful as they are rare, and otherwise introduce some noise when documents are already being processed in a specific publication time-window. For example, the word *today* which appears in most articles of the same day (and would be normalized to that day's date, e.g., "1990.01.12") would gather mentions of a general event type, e.g., *meet*, although, they might not be pointing to the same instance. The employed semantic convention establishes a balance between efficiency and recall of the system. Nevertheless, it sometimes allows clustering of intuitively unrelated actions. In order to enhance the clustering performance in terms of the precision, we have a parameter to give priority to within synset coreference.

Cluster type	Freq.	Avg. content
Singleton	12895	1
Single paragraph	1360	2.36
Single article	807	3.95
Popular	182	2.99

Table 1: Different types of resulting clusters

6.2 Error Analysis

We fed all event mentions from the AQUAINT TimeML corpus into the algorithm exactly in the same way that we did in case of our large news corpora. The algorithm has a few parameters which we set by looking at samples of resulting clusters prior to the measurement on the labeled portion. This is a minimal NLP system given that neither syntactic/semantic dependency of entities to the event head word nor the type of attachment to temporal expressions in the context are taken into account. Nevertheless, we obtain 51.3% precision and 55.6% recall for the pair-wise coreference resolution task on the annotated data. The resulting F-score of 53.4% is comparable with the best F-scores reported in the work of Bejan and Harabagiu (52.1% on ECB for the similar task) while they use a rich linguistic feature set, as well as a more sophisticated clustering method.

Coreference	Total	Related class	Same doc.
True positive	20	100%	25%
True negative	4895	16%	2%
False positive	19	100%	36%
False negative	16	33%	7%
Total	4950	15%	2%

Table 2: Pair-wise decisions

Table 2 shows false positive and negative answers separately. As reflected in the results, positive labels are given only to mention pairs of related classes (headwords need to share a synset, or are related via hypernym and morphosemantic links in WordNet). 36% of positive labels are given to pairs within some article which is expected given that common contextual features are easy to find for them. In such cases, usually linguistic features are needed to resolve participants or the relative temporality of one mention against the other:

a. some people are **born** rich, some are **born** poor.

b. the bullet **bounced** off a cabinet and **ricocheted** into the living room.

In some cases, on the other hand, the disagreement depends on the semantic approach to the definition of identity, and therefore, is more controversial. The human annotator has apparently been more conservative to annotate coreference when the head words of the mentions were a bit different in meaning, whereas the system's decision benefited from some flexibility:

a. the immigration service **decided** the boy should go home. / they made a reasonable decision Wednesday in **ruling** that...
b. if he **goes**, he will immediately **become**...

It is not clear, for example, whether *ruling* is a subevent of the *decision* or exactly the same event. A similar distinction needs to be made in case of the false negative labels. The automatic clustering is not able to detect coreference mostly in case of sparse context, where enough information is not available to resolve the similarity. That is why false negative happens more frequently for mentions coming from different articles (specifically paragraphs sharing few named entities) and only 7% of the time when they happen within a document:

a. the Clinton administration has pushed for the boy's **return**. / his son said he didn't want to **go**.

Sparse context results either in the creation of a singleton cluster for the mention or careless assignment to some wrong cluster, which in the future would decrease the chance of meeting coreferent mentions. False negatives happening for mentions of unrelated semantic classes are due to the missing links between *possibly synonym* words in WordNet, one of the issues that need to be investigated and cured in the future work.

7 Conclusion

This paper presented a variety of material concerning event coreference resolution:

1. A general ontology is explained that can be employed in different studies on events.
2. An algorithm is designed, regardingly, to gather coreferential event in a large corpus.
3. A set of event mentions in AQUAINT TimeML is annotated with pair-wise coreference tags within and between topics[10].
4. An implementation of the method considering simple and scalable features is tested on real data and the annotated corpus.
5. Finally, we performed an error analysis of the automatically assigned labels to identify future directions.

Separating the semantic layer definition of coreference from textual attribution of event mentions has two benefits in our framework. First, it provides us with an efficient partitioning procedure to reduce the search space. Second, it makes the model flexible to allow for different possible semantic conventions which could vary from one application to another. Our adaptation of WordNet synsets allows for integrative future extension of the model — e.g., to capture metaphorical and subevent relations based on `Methonymy` and `Entailment` links. The intuition of using named entities for identification of important real-world events resulted in balanced precision and recall on the test data. In the future, we would like to investigate the effect of linguistic features on improving the performance of the algorithm. In particular, it would be interesting to see whether exact specification of event head arguments would outperform the vague attribution with related entities. The state-of-the-art result in the supervised predicate alignment approach is a hint for rich linguistic features to be helpful (Wolfe et al., 2013). On the other hand, depending on the adapted event identity definition, coreferential events might not really share identical arguments (Hasler and Orasan, 2009). There are differences between real data collections and the available annotated corpora, including ours, which needs to be investigated as well. For example, small collections do not include enough same-class event mentions pointing to different event instances, and it brings about unrealistic evaluations. Furthermore, annotation guidelines are usually biased towards a specific theory of event identity which affect the resulting data in one way or another. Some applications demand different semantic conventions perhaps with broader/narrower definition of identity. This is a dilemma that needs to be resolved through more theoretical studies in touch with real world problems such as the one we introduced in this paper.

[10]The annotation is available at: http://www.coli.uni-saarland.de/~fatemeh/resources.htm

References

Bejan, C. A. and Harabagiu, S. (2010). Unsupervised event coreference resolution with rich linguistic features. In *Proceedings of the 48th Annual Meeting of the Association for Computational Linguistics*, pages 1412–1422. Association for Computational Linguistics.

Blessing, A., Sonntag, J., Kliche, F., Heid, U., Kuhn, J., and Stede, M. (2013). Towards a tool for interactive concept building for large scale analysis in the humanities. In *Proceedings of the 7th Workshop on Language Technology for Cultural Heritage, Social Sciences, and Humanities*, pages 55–64, Sofia, Bulgaria. Association for Computational Linguistics.

Chang, A. X. and Manning, C. (2012). Sutime: A library for recognizing and normalizing time expressions. In *LREC*, pages 3735–3740.

Chen, Z. and Ji, H. (2009). Graph-based event coreference resolution. In *Proceedings of the 2009 Workshop on Graph-based Methods for Natural Language Processing*, pages 54–57. Association for Computational Linguistics.

Cybulska, A. and Vossen, P. (2013). Semantic relations between events and their time, locations and participants for event coreference resolution. In *RANLP*, volume 2013, page 8.

Cybulska, A. and Vossen, P. (2014). Guidelines for ecb+ annotation of events and their coreference. Technical report, Technical Report NWR-2014-1, VU University Amsterdam.

Davidson, D. (1969). The individuation of events. In *Essays in honor of Carl G. Hempel*, pages 216–234. Springer.

Fellbaum, C. (1999). *WordNet*. Wiley Online Library.

Fillmore, C. J., Johnson, C. R., and Petruck, M. R. (2003). Background to framenet. *International journal of lexicography*, 16(3):235–250.

Finlayson, M. A. (2014). Java libraries for accessing the princeton wordnet: Comparison and evaluation. In *Proceedings of the 7th Global Wordnet Conference*, pages 78–85.

Fokkens, A., van Erp, M., Vossen, P., Tonelli, S., van Hage, W. R., SynerScope, B., Serafini, L., Sprugnoli, R., and Hoeksema, J. (2013). Gaf: A grounded annotation framework for events. In *NAACL HLT*, volume 2013, page 11.

Hasler, L. and Orasan, C. (2009). Do coreferential arguments make event mentions coreferential. In *Proc. the 7th Discourse Anaphora and Anaphor Resolution Colloquium (DAARC 2009)*.

Hobbs, J. and Pustejovsky, J. (2003). Annotating and reasoning about time and events. In *Proceedings of AAAI Spring Symposium on Logical Formalizations of Commonsense Reasoning*.

Hovy, E., Mitamura, T., and Palmer, M. (2013a). The 1st workshop on events: Definition, detection, coreference, and representation.

Hovy, E., Mitamura, T., Verdejo, F., Araki, J., and Philpot, A. (2013b). Events are not simple: Identity, non-identity, and quasi-identity. *NAACL HLT 2013*, page 21.

Klyne, G. and Carroll, J. J. (2004). Resource description framework (rdf): Concepts and abstract syntax. w3c recommendation, 10 feb. 2004.

Lee, H., Recasens, M., Chang, A., Surdeanu, M., and Jurafsky, D. (2012). Joint entity and event coreference resolution across documents. In *Proceedings of the 2012 Joint Conference on Empirical Methods in Natural Language Processing and Computational Natural Language Learning*, pages 489–500. Association for Computational Linguistics.

Ogren, P. V., Wetzler, P. G., and Bethard, S. J. (2008). Cleartk: A uima toolkit for statistical natural language processing. *Towards Enhanced Interoperability for Large HLT Systems: UIMA for NLP*, 32.

Pivovarova, L., Huttunen, S., and Yangarber, R. (2013). Event representation across genre. *NAACL HLT 2013*, page 29.

Rao, D., McNamee, P., and Dredze, M. (2010). Streaming cross document entity coreference resolution. In *Proceedings of the 23rd International Conference on Computational Linguistics: Posters*, pages 1050–1058. Association for Computational Linguistics.

Roth, M. and Frank, A. (2012). Aligning predicate argument structures in monolingual comparable texts: A new corpus for a new task. In *Proceedings of the First Joint Conference on Lexical and Computational Semantics-Volume 1: Proceedings of the main conference and the shared task, and Volume 2: Proceedings of the Sixth International Workshop on Semantic Evaluation*, pages 218–227. Association for Computational Linguistics.

Shaw, R. (2013). A semantic tool for historical events. *NAACL HLT 2013*, page 38.

UzZaman, N., Llorens, H., Derczynski, L., Verhagen, M., Allen, J., and Pustejovsky, J. (2013). Semeval-2013 task 1: Tempeval-3: Evaluating time expressions, events, and temporal relations. In *Second joint conference on lexical and computational semantics (* SEM)*, volume 2, pages 1–9.

Wolfe, T., Van Durme, B., Dredze, M., Andrews, N., Beller, C., Callison-Burch, C., DeYoung, J., Snyder, J., Weese, J., Xu, T., et al. (2013). Parma: A predicate argument aligner.

A Comparison of the Events and Relations Across ACE, ERE, TAC-KBP, and FrameNet Annotation Standards

Jacqueline Aguilar and **Charley Beller** and **Paul McNamee** and **Benjamin Van Durme**
Human Language Technology Center of Excellence
Johns Hopkins University
Baltimore, MD, USA

Stephanie Strassel and **Zhiyi Song** and **Joe Ellis**
University of Pennsylvania
Linguistic Data Consortium (LDC)
Philadelphia, PA, USA

Abstract

The resurgence of effort within computational semantics has led to increased interest in various types of relation extraction and semantic parsing. While various manually annotated resources exist for enabling this work, these materials have been developed with different standards and goals in mind. In an effort to develop better general understanding across these resources, we provide a summary overview of the standards underlying ACE, ERE, TAC-KBP Slot-filling, and FrameNet.

1 Overview

ACE and ERE are comprehensive annotation standards that aim to consistently annotate Entities, Events, and Relations within a variety of documents. The ACE (Automatic Content Extraction) standard was developed by NIST in 1999 and has evolved over time to support different evaluation cycles, the last evaluation having occurred in 2008. The ERE (Entities, Relations, Events) standard was created under the DARPA DEFT program as a lighter-weight version of ACE with the goal of making annotation easier, and more consistent across annotators. ERE attempts to achieve this goal by consolidating some of the annotation type distinctions that were found to be the most problematic in ACE, as well as removing some more complex annotation features.

This paper provides an overview of the relationship between these two standards and compares them to the more restricted standard of the TAC-KBP slot-filling task and the more expansive standard of FrameNet. Sections 3 and 4 examine Relations and Events in the ACE/ERE standards, section 5 looks at TAC-KBP slot-filling, and section 6 compares FrameNet to the other standards.

2 ACE and ERE Entity Tagging

Many of the differences in Relations and Events annotation across the ACE and ERE standards stem from differences in entity mention tagging. This is simply because Relation and Event tagging relies on the distinctions established in the entity tagging portion of the annotation process. For example, since ERE collapses the ACE *Facility* and *Location* Types, any ACE Relation or Event that relied on that distinction is revised in ERE. These top-level differences are worth keeping in mind when considering how Events and Relations tagging is approached in ACE and ERE:

- Type Inventory: ACE and ERE share the *Person*, *Organization*, *Geo-Political Entity*, and *Location* Types. ACE has two additional Types: *Vehicle* and *Weapon*. ERE does not account for these Types and collapses the *Facility* and *Location* Types into *Location*. ERE also includes a *Title* Type to address titles, honorifics, roles, and professions (Linguistic Data Consortium, 2006; Linguistic Data Consortium, 2013a).
- Subtype Annotation: ACE further classifies entity mentions by including Subtypes for each determined Type; if the entity does not fit into any Subtype, it is not annotated. ERE annotation does not include any Subtypes.
- Entity Classes: In addition to Subtype, ACE also classifies each entity mention according

Proceedings of the 2nd Workshop on EVENTS: Definition, Detection, Coreference, and Representation, pages 45–53,
Baltimore, Maryland, USA, June 22-27, 2014.

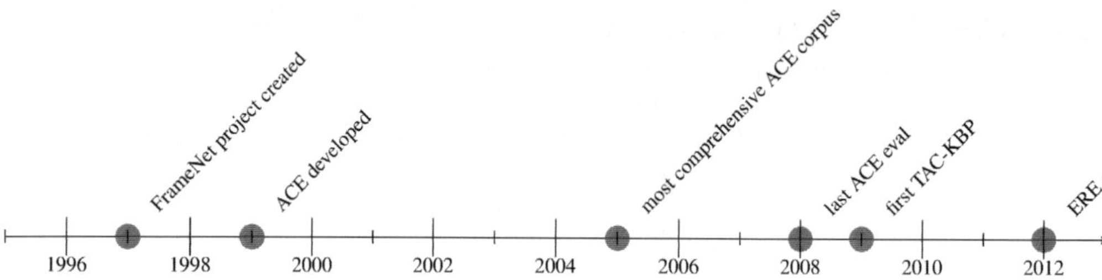

Figure 1: Important Dates for the ACE, ERE, TAC-KBP, and FrameNet Standards

to entity class (Specific, Generic, Attributive, and Underspecified).

- Taggability: ACE tags Attributive, Generic, Specific, and Underspecified entity mentions. ERE only tags Specific entity mentions.
- Extents and Heads: ACE marks the full noun phrase of an entity mention and tags a head word. ERE handles tagging based on the mention level of an entity; in Name mentions (NAM) the name is the extent, in Nominal mentions (NOM) the full noun phrase is the extent, in Pronoun mentions (PRO) the pronoun is the extent.
- Tags: ERE only specifies Type and Mention level (NAM, NOM, PRO). ACE specifies Type, Subtype, Entity Class (Attributive, Generic, Specific, Underspecified), and Mention Level (NAM, NOM, PRO, Headless).

3 Relations in ACE and ERE

In the ACE and ERE annotation models, the goal of the Relations task is to detect and characterize *relations* of the targeted *types* between *entities* (Linguistic Data Consortium, 2008; Linguistic Data Consortium, 2013c). The purpose of this task is to extract a representation of the meaning of the text, not necessarily tied to underlying syntactic or lexical semantic representations. Both models share similar overarching guidelines for determining what is *taggable*. For relations the differences lie in the absence or presence of additional features, *syntactic classes*, as well as differences in *assertion*, *trigger words*, and minor *subtype* variations.

3.1 Similarities in Relations Annotation

In addition to comprising similar Types (both models include *Physical* and *Part.Whole* Types as well as slightly different Types to address *Affiliation* and *Social* relations) used to characterize each relation, ACE and ERE share important similarities concerning their relation-tagging guidelines. These include:

- Limiting relations to only those expressed in a single sentence
- Tagging only for explicit mention
- No 'promoting' or 'nesting' of taggable entities. In the sentence, *Smith went to a hotel in Brazil*, (Smith, hotel) is a taggable *Physical.Located* relation, but (Smith, Brazil) is not. This is because in order to tag this as such, one would have to promote 'Brazil'.
- Tagging for past and former relations
- Two different Argument slots (Arg1 and Arg2) are provided for each relation to capture the importance of Argument ordering.
- Arguments can be more than one token (although ACE marks the head as well)
- Using 'templates' for each relation Type/Subtype (*e.g.*, in a *Physical.Located* relation, the Person that is located somewhere will always be assigned to Arg1 and the place in which the person is located will always be assigned to Arg2).
- Neither model tags for negative relations
- Both methods contain argument span boundaries. That is, the relations should only include *tagged* entities within the extent of a sentence.

3.2 Differences in Assertion, Modality, and Tense

A primary difference between these two annotation models is a result of ERE only annotating asserted events while ACE also includes hypotheticals. ACE accounts for these cases by including two Modality attributes: ASSERTED and OTHER

(Linguistic Data Consortium, 2008). For example, in the sentence, *We are afraid that Al-Qaeda terrorists will be in Baghdad*, ACE would tag this as an OTHER attribute, where OTHER pertains to situations in "some other world defined by counterfactual constraints elsewhere in the context", whereas ERE would simply not tag a relation in this sentence. Additionally, while both ACE and ERE tag past and former relations, ACE goes further to mark the Tense of each relation by means of four attributes: Past, Future, Present and Unspecified.

3.3 Syntactic Classes

ACE further justifies the tagging of each Relation through Syntactic Classes. The primary function of these classes is to serve as a sanity check on taggability and as an additional constraint for tagging. These classes include: Possessive, Preposition, PreMod, Coordination, Formulaic, Participal, Verbal, Relations Expressed by Verbs, and Other. Syntactic classes are not present in ERE relations annotation.

3.4 Triggers

Explicit trigger words do not exist in ACE relation annotation; instead, the model annotates the full syntactic clause that serves as the 'trigger' for the relation. ERE attempts to minimize the annotated span by allowing for the tagging of an optional trigger word, defined as "the smallest extent of text that indicates a relation Type and Subtype" (Linguistic Data Consortium, 2013c). These triggers are not limited to a single word, but can also be composed of a phrase or any extent of the text that indicates a Type/Subtype relation, left to the discretion of the annotator. It is common for prepositions to be triggers, as in *John is **in** Chicago*. However, sometimes no trigger is needed because the syntax of the sentence is such that it indicates a particular relation Type/Subtype without a word to explicitly signal the relation.

3.5 Types and Subtypes of Relations

There are three types of relations that contain varied Subtypes between ERE and ACE. These are the *Physical*, *Part-Whole*, *Social* and *Affiliation* Types. The differences are a result of ERE collapsing ACE Types and Subtypes into more concise, if less specific, Type groups.

Physical Relation Type Differences The main differences in the handling of the physical relations between ACE and ERE are shown in Table 1. ACE only marks Location for PERSON entities (for Arg1). ERE uses Location for PERSON entities being located somewhere as well as for a geographical location being part of another geographical location. Additionally, ACE includes 'Near' as a Subtype. This is used for when an entity is explicitly near another entity, but neither entity is a part of the other or located in/at the other. ERE does not have an equivalent Subtype to account for this physical relation. Instead, ERE includes 'Origin' as a Subtype. This is used to describe the relation between a PER and an ORG. ACE does not have a *Physical* Type equivalent, but it does account for this type of relation within a separate *General Affiliation* Type and 'Citizen-Resident-Religion-Ethnicity' Subtype.

Part-Whole Relation Differences In Table 2, note that ACE has a 'Geographical' Subtype which captures the location of a FAC, LOC, or GPE in or at, or as part of another FAC, LOC, or GPE. Examples of this would be *India controlled the region* or a phrase such as *the Atlanta area*. ERE does not include this type of annotation option. Instead, ERE tags these regional relations as *Physical.Located*. ACE and ERE do share a 'Subsidiary' Subtype which is defined in both models as a "category to capture the ownership, administrative and other hierarchical relationships between ORGs and/or GPEs" (Linguistic Data Consortium, 2008; Linguistic Data Consortium, 2013c).

Social and Affiliation Relation Differences The most evident discrepancy in relation annotation between the two models lies in the *Social* and *Affiliation* Relation Types and Subtypes. For social relations, ACE and ERE have three Subtypes with similar goals (Business, Family, Unspecified/Lasting-Personal) but ERE has an additional 'Membership' Subtype, as shown in Table 3. ACE addresses all 'Membership' relations in its *Affiliation* Type. ERE also includes the 'Social.Role' Subtype in order to address the *TITLE* entity type, which only applies to ERE. However, both models agree that the arguments for each relation must be PERSON entities and that they should not include relationships implied from interaction between two entities (*e.g., President*

Relation Type	Relation Subtype	ARG1 Type	ARG2 Type
		ERE	
Physical	Located	PER, GPE, LOC	GPE, LOC
Physical	Origin	PER, ORG	GPE, LOC
		ACE	
Physical	Located	PER	FAC, LOC, GPE
Physical	Near	PER, FAC, GPE, LOC	FAC, GPE, LOC

Table 1: Comparison of Permitted Relation Arguments for the *Physical* Type Distinction in the ERE and ACE Guidelines

Relation Type	Relation Subtype	ARG1 Type	ARG2 Type
		ERE	
Part-Whole	Subsidiary	ORG	ORG, GPE
		ACE	
Part-Whole	Geographical	FAC, LOC, GPE	FAC, LOC, GPE
Part-Whole	Subsidiary	ORG	ORG, GPE

Table 2: Comparison of Permitted Relation Arguments for the *Part-Whole* Type and Subtype Distinctions in the ERE and ACE Guidelines

Relation Type	Relation Subtype	ARG1 Type	ARG2 Type
		ERE	
Social	Business	PER	PER
Social	Family	PER	PER
Social	Membership	PER	PER
Social	Role	TTL	PER
Social	Unspecified	PER	PER
		ACE	
Personal-Social	Business	PER	PER
Personal-Social	Family	PER	PER
Personal-Social	Lasting-Personal	PER	PER

Table 3: Comparison of Permitted Relation Arguments for the *Social* Type and Subtype Distinctions in the ERE and ACE Guidelines

Relation Type	Relation Subtype	ARG1 Type	ARG2 Type
		ERE	
Affiliation	Employment/Membership	PER, ORG, GPE	ORG, GPE
Affiliation	Leadership	PER	ORG, GPE
		ACE	
ORG-Affiliation	Employment	PER	ORG, GPE
ORG-Affiliation	Ownership	PER	ORG
ORG-Affiliation	Founder	PER, ORG	ORG, GPE
ORG-Affiliation	Student-Alum	PER	ORG.Educational
ORG-Affiliation	Sports-Affiliation	PER	ORG
ORG-Affiliation	Investor-Shareholder	PER, ORG, GPE	ORG, GPE
ORG-Affiliation	Membership	PER, ORG, GPE	ORG
Agent-Artifact	User-Owner-Inventor-Manufacturer	PER, ORG, GPE	FAC
Gen-Affiliation	Citizen-Resident-Religion-Ethnicity	PER	PER.Group, LOC, GPE, ORG
Gen-Affiliation	Org-Location-Origin	ORG	LOC, GPE

Table 4: Comparison of Permitted Relation Arguments for the *Affiliation* Type and Subtype Distinctions in the ERE and ACE Guidelines

Clinton met with Yasser Arafat last week would not be considered a social relation).

As for the differences in affiliation relations, ACE includes many Subtype possibilities which can more accurately represent affiliation, whereas ERE only observes two Affiliation Subtype options (Table 4).

4 Events in ACE and ERE

Events in both annotation methods are defined as 'specific occurrences', involving 'specific participants' (Linguistic Data Consortium, 2005; Linguistic Data Consortium, 2013b). The primary goal of Event tagging is to detect and characterize events that include tagged entities. The central Event tagging difference between ACE and ERE is the level of specificity present in ACE, whereas ERE tends to collapse tags for a more simplified approach.

4.1 Event Tagging Similarities

Both annotation schemas annotate the same exact Event Types: LIFE, MOVEMENT, TRANSACTION, BUSINESS, CONFLICT, CONTACT, PERSONNEL, and JUSTICE events. Both annotation ontologies also include 33 Subtypes for each Type. Furthermore, both rely on the expression of an occurrence through the use of a 'Trigger'. ACE, however, restricts the trigger to be a single word that most clearly expresses the event occurrence (usually a main verb), while ERE allows for the trigger to be a word or a phrase that instantiates the event (Linguistic Data Consortium, 2005; Linguistic Data Consortium, 2013b). Both methods annotate modifiers when they trigger events as well as anaphors, when they refer to previously mentioned events. Furthermore, when there is any ambiguity about which trigger to select, both methods have similar rules established, such as the Stand-Alone Noun Rule (*In cases where more than one trigger is possible, the noun that can be used by itself to refer to the event will be selected*) and the Stand-Alone Adjective Rule (*Whenever a verb and an adjective are used together to express the occurrence of an Event, the adjective will be chosen as the trigger whenever it can stand-alone to express the resulting state brought about by the Event*). Additionally, both annotation guidelines agree on the following:

- Tagging of Resultative Events (states that result from taggable Events)
- Nominalized Events are tagged as regular events
- Reported Events are **not** tagged
- Implicit events are **not** tagged
- Light verbs are **not** tagged
- Coreferential Events are tagged
- Tagging of multi-part triggers (both parts are tagged only if they are contiguous)

4.2 Event Tagging Differences

One of the more general differences between ERE and ACE Event tagging is the way in which each model addresses *Event Extent*. ACE defines the extent as always being the 'entire sentence within which the Event is described' (Linguistic Data Consortium, 2005). In ERE, the extent is the entire document unless an event is coreferenced (in which case, the extent is defined as the 'span of a document from the first trigger for a particular event to the next trigger for a particular event.' This signifies that the span can cross sentence boundaries). Unlike ACE, ERE does not delve into indicating Polarity, Tense, Genericity, and Modality. ERE simplifies any annotator confusion engendered by these features by simply not tagging negative, future, hypothetical, conditional, uncertain or generic events (although it does tag for past events). While ERE only tags attested Events, ACE allows for irrealis events, and includes attributes for marking them as such: Believed Events; Hypothetical Events; Commanded and Requested Events; Threatened, Proposed and Discussed Events; Desired Events; Promised Events; and Otherwise Unclear Constructions. Additionally both ERE and ACE tag Event arguments as long as the arguments occur within the event mention extent (another way of saying that a taggable Event argument will occur in the same sentence as the trigger word for its Event). However, ERE and ACE have a diverging approach to argument tagging:

- ERE is limited to pre-specified arguments for each event and relation subtype. The possible arguments for ACE are: Event participants (limited to pre-specified roles for each event type); Event-specific attributes that are associated with a particular event type (*e.g.*, the victim of an attack); and General event attributes that can apply to most or all event types (*e.g.*, time, place).

- ACE tags arguments regardless of modal certainty of their involvement in the event. ERE only tags asserted participants in the event.
- The full noun phrase is marked in both ERE and ACE arguments, but the head is only specified in ACE. This is because ACE handles entity annotation slightly differently than ERE does; ACE marks the full noun phrase with a head word for entity mention, and ERE treats mentions differently based on their syntactic features (for named or pronominal entity mentions the name or pronominal itself is marked, whereas for nominal mentions the full noun phrase is marked).

Event Type and Subtype Differences Both annotation methods have almost identical Event Type and Subtype categories. The only differences between both are present in the Contact and Movement Event Types.

A minor distinction in Subtype exists as a result of the types of entities that can be transported within the Movement Type category. In ACE, ARTIFACT entities (WEAPON or VEHICLE) as well as PERSON entities can be transported, whereas in ERE, only PERSON entities can be transported. The difference between the Phone-Write and Communicate Subtypes merely lies in the definition. Both Subtypes are the default Subtype to cover all Contact events where a 'face-to-face' meeting between sender and receiver is not explicitly stated. In ACE, this contact is limited to written or telephone communication where at least two parties are specified to make this event subtype less open-ended. In ERE, this requirement is simply widened to comprise electronic communication as well, explicitly including those via internet channels (*e.g.,* Skype).

5 TAC-KBP

After the final ACE evaluation in 2008 there was interest in the community to form an evaluation explicitly focused on knowledge bases (KBs) created from the output of extraction systems. NIST had recently started the Text Analysis Conference series for related NLP tasks such as Recognizing Textual Entailment, Summarization, and Question Answering. In 2009 the first Knowledge Base Population track (TAC-KBP) was held featuring two initial tasks: (a) Entity Linking — linking entities to KB entities, and (b) Slot Filling — adding information to entity profiles that is missing from the KB (McNamee et al., 2010). Due to its generous license and large scale, a snapshot of English Wikipedia from late 2008 has been used as the reference KB in the TAC-KBP evaluations.

5.1 Slot Filling Overview

Unlike ACE and ERE, Slot Filling does not have as its primary goal the annotation of text. Rather, the aim is to identify knowledge nuggets about a focal named entity using a fixed inventory of relations and attributes. For example, given a focal entity such as former Ukrainian prime minister Yulia Tymoshenko, the task is to identify attributes such as schools she attended, occupations, and immediate family members. This is the same sort of information commonly listed about prominent people in Wikipedia Infoboxes and in derivative databases such as FreeBase and DBpedia.

Consequently, Slot Filling is somewhat of a hybrid between relation extraction and question answering — slot fills can be considered as the correct responses to a fixed set of questions. The relations and attributes used in the 2013 task are presented in Table 5.

5.2 Differences with ACE-style relation extraction

Slot Filling in TAC-KBP differs from extraction in ACE and ERE in several significant ways:

- information is sought for *named* entities, chiefly PERs and ORGs;
- the focus is on values not mentions;
- assessment is more like QA; and,
- events are handled as uncorrelated slots

In traditional IE evaluation, there was an implicit skew towards highly attested information such as $leader(Bush, US)$, or $capital(Paris, France)$. In contrast, TAC-KBP gives full credit for finding a single instance of a correct fill instead of every attestation of that fact.

Slot Filling assessment is somewhat simpler than IE annotation. The assessor must decide if provenance text is supportive of a posited fact about the focal entity instead of annotating a document with all evidenced relations and events for any entity. For clarity and to increase assessor agreement, guidelines have been developed to justify when a posited relation is deemed adequately supported from text. Additionally, the problem of

Relations		Attributes	
per:children	org:shareholders	per:alternate_names	org:alternate_names
per:other_family	org:founded_by	per:date_of_birth	org:political_religious_affiliation
per:parents	org:top_members_employees	per:age	org:number_of_employees_members
per:siblings	org:member_of	per:origin	org:date_founded
per:spouse	org:members	per:date_of_death	org:date_dissolved
per:employee_or_member_of	org:parents	per:cause_of_death	org:website
per:schools_attended	org:subsidiaries	per:title	
per:city_of_birth	org:city_of_headquarters	per:religion	
per:stateorprovince_of_birth	org:stateorprovince_of_headquarters	per:charges	
per:country_of_birth	org:country_of_headquarters		
per:cities_of_residence			
per:statesorprovinces_of_residence			
per:countries_of_residence			
per:city_of_death			
per:stateorprovince_of_death			
per:country_of_death			

Table 5: Relation and attributes for PERs and ORGs.

slot value equivalence becomes an issue - a system should be penalized for redundantly asserting that a person has four children named Tim, Beth, Timothy, and Elizabeth, or that a person is both a cardiologist and a doctor.

Rather than explicitly modeling events, TAC-KBP created relations that capture events, more in line with the notion of Infobox filling or question answering (McNamee et al., 2010). For example, instead of a criminal event, there is a slot fill for charges brought against an entity. Instead of a founding event, there are slots like org:founded_by (who) and org:date_founded (when). Thus a statement that "Jobs is the founder and CEO of Apple" is every bit as useful for the org:founded_by relation as "Jobs founded Apple in 1976." even though the date is not included in the former sentence.

5.3 Additional tasks

Starting in 2012 TAC-KBP introduced the "Cold Start" task, which is to literally produce a KB based on the Slot Filling schema. To date, Cold Start KBs have been built from collections of O(50,000) documents, and due to their large size, they are assessed by sampling. There is also an event argument detection evaluation in KBP planned for 2014.

Other TAC-KBP tasks have been introduced including determining the timeline when dynamic slot fills are valid (*e.g.,* CEO of Microsoft), and targeted sentiment.

6 FrameNet

The FrameNet project has rather different motivations than either ACE/ERE or TAC-KBP, but shares with them a goal of capturing information about events and relations in text. FrameNet stems from Charles Fillmore's linguistic and lexicographic theory of Frame Semantics (Fillmore, 1976; Fillmore, 1982). Frames are descriptions of event (or state) types and contain information about event participants (*frame elements*), information as to how event types relate to each other (*frame relations*), and information about which words or multi-word expressions can trigger a given frame (*lexical units*).

FrameNet is designed with text annotation in mind, but unlike ACE/ERE it prioritizes lexicographic and linguistic completeness over ease of annotation. As a result Frames tend to be much finer grained than ACE/ERE events, and are more numerous by an order of magnitude. The Berkeley FrameNet Project (Baker et al., 1998) was developed as a machine readable database of distinct frames and lexical units (words and multi-word constructions) that were known to trigger specific frames.[1] FrameNet 1.5 includes 1020 identified frames and 11830 lexical units.

One of the most widespread uses of FrameNet has been as a resource for Semantic Role Labeling (SRL) (Gildea and Jurafsky, 2002). FrameNet related SRL was promoted as a task by the SENSEVAL-3 workshop (Litkowski, 2004), and the SemEval-2007 workshop (Baker et al., 2007). (Das et al., 2010) is a current system for automatic FrameNet annotation.

The relation and attribute types of TAC-KBP and the relation and event types in the ACE/ERE standards can be mapped to FrameNet frames. The mapping is complicated by two factors. The first is that FrameNet frames are generally more fine-grained than the ACE/ERE categories. As a result the mapping is sometimes one-to-many. For example, the ERE relation **Af-**

[1]This database is accessible via webpage (`https://framenet.icsi.berkeley.edu/fndrupal/`) and as a collection of XML files by request.

Relations

FrameNet	ACE	ERE	TAC-KBP
Kinship	Personal-Social.Family	Social.Family	per:children per:other_family per:parents per:siblings per:spouse
Being_Employed Membership	ORG-Affiliation.Employment	Affiliation.Employment/Membership	per:employee_or_member_of org:member_of
Being_Located	Physical.Located	Physical.Located	org:city_of_headquarters org:stateorprovince_of_headquarters org:country_of_headquarters

Events

FrameNet	ACE	ERE
Contacting	Phone-Write	Communicate
Extradition	Justice-Extradition	Justice-Extradition
Attack	Conflict-Attack	Conflict-Attack
Being_Born	Life-Be_Born	Life-Be_Born

Attributes

FrameNet	TAC-KBP
Being_Named	per:alternate_names
Age	per:age

Table 6: Rough mappings between subsets of FrameNet, ACE, ERE, and TAC-KBP

filiation.Employment/Membership covers both the **Being_Employed** frame and the **Membership** frame. At the same time, while TAC-KBP has only a handful of relations relative to FrameNet, some of these relations are more fine-grained than the analogous frames or ACE/ERE relations. For example, the frame **Kinship**, which maps to the single ERE relation **Social.Family**, maps to five TAC-KBP relations, and the **Being_Located**, which maps to the ACE/ERE relation **Being.Located**, maps to three TAC-KBP relations. Rough mappings from a selection of relations, events, and attributes are given in Table 6.

The second complication arises from the fact that FrameNet frames are more complex objects than ERE/ACE events, and considerably more complex than TAC-KBP relations. Rather than the two entities related via a TAC-KBP or ACE/ERE relation, some frames have upwards of 20 frame elements. Table 7 shows in detail the mapping between frame elements in the Extradition frame and ACE's and ERE's Justice-Extradition events. The "core" frame elements map exactly to the ERE event, the remaining two arguments in the ACE event map to two non-core frame elements, and the frame includes several more non-core elements with no analogue in either ACE or ERE standards.

FrameNet	ACE	ERE
Authorities	Agent-Arg	Agent-Arg
Crime_jursidiction	Destination-Arg	Destination-Arg
Current_jursidiction	Origin-Arg	Origin-Arg
Suspect	Person-Arg	Person-Arg
Reason	Crime-Arg	
Time	Time-Arg	
Legal_Basis		
Manner		
Means		
Place		
Purpose		
Depictive		

Table 7: Mapping between frame elements of Extradition (FrameNet), and arguments of Justice-Extradition (ACE/ERE): A line divides core frame elements (above) from non-core (below).

7 Conclusion

The ACE and ERE annotation schemas have closely related goals of identifying similar information across various possible types of documents, though their approaches differ due to separate goals regarding scope and replicability. ERE differs from ACE in collapsing different Type distinctions and in removing annotation features in order to eliminate annotator confusion and to improve consistency, efficiency, and higher inter-annotator agreement. TAC-KPB slot-filling shares some goals with ACE/ERE, but is wholly focused on a set collection of questions (slots to be filled) concerning entities to the extent that there is no explicit modeling of events. At the other extreme, FrameNet seeks to capture the full range of linguistic and lexicographic variation in event representations in text. In general, all events, relations, and attributes that can be represented by ACE/ERE and TAC-KBP standards can be mapped to FrameNet representations, though adjustments need to be made for granularity of event/relation types and granularity of arguments.

Acknowledgements

This material is partially based on research sponsored by the NSF under grant IIS-1249516 and DARPA under agreement number FA8750-13-2-0017 (the DEFT program).

References

Collin F Baker, Charles J Fillmore, and John B Lowe. 1998. The berkeley framenet project. In *Proceedings of the 17th international conference on Computational linguistics-Volume 1*, pages 86–90. Association for Computational Linguistics.

Collin Baker, Michael Ellsworth, and Katrin Erk. 2007. Semeval-2007 task 19: Frame semantic structure extraction. In *Proceedings of the Fourth International Workshop on Semantic Evaluations (SemEval-2007)*, pages 99–104, Prague, Czech Republic, June. Association for Computational Linguistics.

Dipanjan Das, Nathan Schneider, Desai Chen, and Noah A Smith. 2010. Probabilistic frame-semantic parsing. In *Proceedings of NAACL-HLT*, pages 948–956. Association for Computational Linguistics.

George Doddington, Alexis Mitchell, Mark Przybocki, Lancec Ramshaw, Stephanie Strassel, and Ralph Weischedel. 2004. The automatic content extraction (ace) program- tasks, data, and evaluation. In *Proceedings of LREC 2004: Fourth International Conference on Language Resources and Evaluation*, Lisbon, May 24-30.

Charles J Fillmore. 1976. Frame semantics and the nature of language. *Annals of the New York Academy of Sciences*, 280(1):20–32.

Charles Fillmore. 1982. Frame semantics. In *Linguistics in the morning calm*, pages 111–137. Hanshin Publishing Co.

Daniel Gildea and Daniel Jurafsky. 2002. Automatic labeling of semantic roles. *Computational linguistics*, 28(3):245–288.

Linguistic Data Consortium. 2005. ACE (automatic content extraction) English annotation guidelines for events. `https://www.ldc.upenn.edu/collaborations/past-projects/ace`. Version 5.4.3 2005.07.01.

Linguistic Data Consortium. 2006. ACE (automatic content extraction) English annotation guidelines for entities. `https://www.ldc.upenn.edu/collaborations/past-projects/ace`, Version 5.6.6 2006.08.01.

Linguistic Data Consortium. 2008. ACE (automatic content extraction) English annotation guidelines for relations. `https://www.ldc.upenn.edu/collaborations/past-projects/ace`. Version 6.0 2008.01.07.

Linguistic Data Consortium. 2013a. DEFT ERE annotation guidelines: Entities v1.1, 05.17.2013.

Linguistic Data Consortium. 2013b. DEFT ERE annotation guidelines: Events v1.1. 05.17.2013.

Linguistic Data Consortium. 2013c. DEFT ERE annotation guidelines: Relations v1.1. 05.17.2013.

Ken Litkowski. 2004. Senseval-3 task: Automatic labeling of semantic roles. In Rada Mihalcea and Phil Edmonds, editors, *Senseval-3: Third International Workshop on the Evaluation of Systems for the Semantic Analysis of Text*, pages 9–12, Barcelona, Spain, July. Association for Computational Linguistics.

Paul McNamee, Hoa Trang Dang, Heather Simpson, Patrick Schone, and Stephanie Strassel. 2010. An evaluation of technologies for knowledge base population. In *Proceedings of LREC*.

Is the Stanford Dependency Representation Semantic?

Rachel Rudinger[1] and **Benjamin Van Durme**[1,2]
Center for Language and Speech Processing[1]
Human Language Technology Center of Excellence[2]
Johns Hopkins University
rudinger@jhu.edu, vandurme@cs.jhu.edu

Abstract

The Stanford Dependencies are a deep syntactic representation that are widely used for semantic tasks, like Recognizing Textual Entailment. But do they capture all of the semantic information a meaning representation ought to convey? This paper explores this question by investigating the feasibility of mapping Stanford dependency parses to Hobbsian Logical Form, a practical, event-theoretic semantic representation, using only a set of deterministic rules. Although we find that such a mapping is possible in a large number of cases, we also find cases for which such a mapping seems to require information beyond what the Stanford Dependencies encode. These cases shed light on the kinds of semantic information that are and are not present in the Stanford Dependencies.

1 Introduction

The Stanford dependency parser (De Marneffe et al., 2006) provides "deep" syntactic analysis of natural language by layering a set of hand-written post-processing rules on top of Stanford's statistical constituency parser (Klein and Manning, 2003). Stanford dependency parses are commonly used as a semantic representation in natural language understanding and inference systems.[1] For example, they have been used as a basic meaning representation for the Recognizing Textual Entailment task proposed by Dagan et al. (2005), such as by Haghighi et al. (2005) or MacCartney (2009) and in other inference systems (Chambers et al., 2007; MacCartney, 2009).

Because of their popular use as a semantic representation, it is important to ask whether the Stanford Dependencies do, in fact, encode the kind of information that ought to be present in a versatile semantic form. This paper explores this question by attempting to map the Stanford Dependencies into Hobbsian Logical Form (henceforth, HLF), a neo-Davidsonian semantic representation designed for practical use (Hobbs, 1985). Our approach is to layer a set of hand-written rules on top of the Stanford Dependencies to further transform the representation into HLFs. This approach is a natural extension of the Stanford Dependencies which are, themselves, derived from manually engineered post-processing routines.

The aim of this paper is neither to demonstrate the semantic completeness of the Stanford Dependencies, nor to exhaustively enumerate their semantic deficiencies. Indeed, to do so would be to presuppose HLF as an entirely complete semantic representation, or, a perfect semantic standard against which to compare the Stanford Dependencies. We make no such claim. Rather, our intent is to provide a qualitative discussion of the Stanford Dependencies as a semantic resource through the lens of this HLF mapping task. It is only necessary that HLF capture some subset of important semantic phenomena to make this exercise meaningful.

Our results indicate that in a number of cases, it is, in fact, possible to directly derive HLFs from Stanford dependency parses. At the same time, however, we also find difficult-to-map phenomena that reveal inherent limitations of the dependencies as a meaning representation.

2 Background

This section provides a brief overview of the HLF and Stanford dependency formalisms.

2.1 Hobbsian Logical Form

The key insight of event-theoretic semantic representations is the *reification* of events (Davidson, 1967), or, treating events as entities in the world. As a logical, first-order representation, Hobbsian

[1]Statement presented by Chris Manning at the *SEM 2013 Panel on Language Understanding http://nlpers.blogspot.com/2013/07/the-sem-2013-panel-on-language.html.

Proceedings of the 2nd Workshop on EVENTS: Definition, Detection, Coreference, and Representation, pages 54–58,
Baltimore, Maryland, USA, June 22-27, 2014.

Logical Form (Hobbs, 1985) employs this approach by allowing for the reification of *any* predicate into an event variable. Specifically, for any predicate $p(x_1, \cdots, x_n)$, there is a corresponding predicate, $p'(E, x_1, \cdots, x_n)$, where E refers to the predicate (or event) $p(x_1, \cdots, x_n)$. The reified predicates are related to their non-reified forms with the following axiom schema:

$$(\forall x_1 \cdots x_n) p(x_1 \cdots x_n) \leftrightarrow (\exists e) Exist(e) \wedge p'(e, x_1 \cdots x_n)$$

In HLF, "A boy runs" would be represented as:

$$(\exists e, x) Exist(e) \wedge run'(e, x) \wedge boy(x)$$

and the sentence "A boy wants to build a boat quickly" (Hobbs, 1985) would be represented as:

$$(\exists e_1, e_2, e_3, x, y) Exist(e_1) \wedge want'(e_1, x, e_2) \wedge quick'(e_2, e_3) \wedge build'(e_3, x, y) \wedge boy(x) \wedge boat(y)$$

2.2 Stanford Dependencies

A Stanford dependency parse is a set of triples consisting of two tokens (a *governor* and a *dependent*), and a labeled syntactic or semantic relation between the two tokens. Parses can be rendered as labeled, directed graphs, as in Figure 1. Note that this paper assumes the *collapsed* version of the Stanford Dependencies.[2]

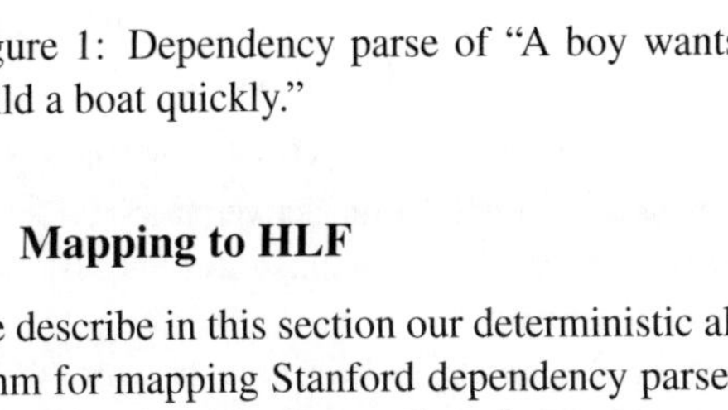

Figure 1: Dependency parse of "A boy wants to build a boat quickly."

3 Mapping to HLF

We describe in this section our deterministic algorithm for mapping Stanford dependency parses to HLF. The algorithm proceeds in four stages: *event extraction*, *argument identification*, *predicate-argument assignment*, and *formula construction*. We demonstrate these steps on the above example sentence "A boy wants to build a boat quickly."[3] The rule-based algorithm operates on the sentence level and is purely a function of the dependency parse or other trivially extractible information, such as capitalization.

3.1 Event Extraction

The first step is to identify the set of event predicates that will appear in the final HLF and assign an event variable to each. Most predicates are generated by a single token in the sentence (e.g., the main verb). For each token t in the sentence, an event (e_i, p_t) (where e_i is the event variable and p_t is the predicate) is added to the set of events if any of the following conditions are met:

1. t is the dependent of the relation $root$, $ccomp$, $xcomp$, $advcl$, $advmod$, or $partmod$.

2. t is the governor of the relation $nsubj$, $dobj$, $ccomp$, $xcomp$, $xsubj$, $advcl$, $nsubjpass$, or $agent$.

Furthermore, an event (e_i, p_r) is added for any triple (rel, gov, dep) where rel is prefixed with "prep_" (e.g., $prep\_to$, $prep\_from$, $prep\_by$, etc.).

Applying this step to our example sentence "A boy wants to build a boat quickly." yields the following set:

$$(e_1, wants), (e_2, quickly), (e_3, build)$$

3.2 Argument Identification

Next, the set of entities that will serve as predicate arguments are identified. Crucially, this set will include some event variables generated in the previous step. For each token, t, an argument (x_i, t) is added to the set of arguments if one of the following conditions is met:

1. t is the dependent of the relation $nsubj$, $xsubj$, $dobj$, $ccomp$, $xcomp$, $nsubjpass$, $agent$, or $iobj$.

2. t is the governor of the relation $advcl$, $advmod$, or $partmod$.

[2]The collapsed version is more convenient for our purposes, but using the uncollapsed version would not significantly affect our results.

[3]Hobbs (1985) uses the example sentence "A boy wanted to build a boat quickly."

Applying this step to our example sentence, we get the following argument set:

$$(x_1, boat), (x_2, build), (x_3, boy)$$

Notice that the token *build* has generated both an event predicate and an argument. This is because in our final HLF, *build* will be both an event predicate that takes the arguments *boy* and *boat*, as well as an argument to the intensional predicate *want*.

3.3 Predicate-Argument Assignment

In this stage, arguments are assigned to each predicate. $p_t.arg_i$ denotes the ith argument of predicate p_t and $arg(t)$ denotes the argument associated with token t. For example, $arg(boy) = x_2$ and $arg(quickly) = e_3$. We also say that if the token t_1 governs t_2 by some relation, e.g. $nsubj$, then t_1 $nsubj$-governs t_2, or t_2 $nsubj$-depends on t_1. Note that arg_i refers to any slot past arg_2. Arguments are assigned as follows.

For each predicate p_t (corresponding to token t):

1. If there is a token t' such that t $nsubj$-, $xsubj$-, or $agent$-governs t', then $p_t.arg_1 = arg(t')$.
2. If there is a token t' such that t $dobj$-governs t', then $p_t.arg_2 = arg(t')$.
3. If there is a token t' such that t $nsubjpass$-governs t', then $p_t.arg_i = arg(t')$.
4. If there is a token t' such that t $partmod$-depends on t', then $p_t.arg_2 = arg(t')$.
5. If there is a token t' such that t $iobj$-governs t', then $p_t.arg_i = arg(t')$.
6. If there is a token t' such that t $ccomp$- or $xcomp$-governs t', then $p_t.arg_i = arg(t')$
   (a) UNLESS there is a token t'' such that t' $advmod$-governs t'', in which case $p_t.arg_i = arg(t'')$.
7. If there is a token t' such that t $advmod$- or $advcl$-depends on t', then $p_t.arg_i = arg(t')$.

And for each p_r generated from relation (rel, gov, dep) (i.e. all of the "prep_" relations):

1. $p_r.arg_1 = arg(gov)$
2. $p_r.arg_i = arg(dep)$

After running this stage on our example sentence, the predicate-argument assignments are as follows:

$$wants(x_3, e_2), build(x_3, x_1), quickly(e_3)$$

Each predicate can be directly replaced with its reified forms (i.e., p'):

$$wants'(e_1, x_3, e_2), build'(e_3, x_3, x_1), \\ quickly'(e_2, e_3)$$

Two kinds of non-eventive predicates still need to be formed. First, every entity (x_i, t) that is neither a reified event nor a proper noun, e.g., (x_3, boy), generates a predicate of the form $t(x_i)$. Second, we generate Hobbs's $Exist$ predicate, which identifies which event actually occurs in the "real world." This is simply the event generated by the dependent of the $root$ relation.

3.4 Formula Construction

In this stage, the final HLF is pieced together. We join all of the predicates formed above with the *and* conjunction, and existentially quantify over every variable found therein. For our example sentence, the resulting HLF is:

A boy wants to build a boat quickly.
$(\exists e_1, e_2, e_3, x_1, x_3)[Exist(e_1) \wedge boat(x_1) \wedge boy(x_3) \wedge wants'(e_1, x_3, e_2) \wedge build'(e_3, x_3, x_1) \wedge quickly'(e_2, e_3)]$

4 Analysis of Results

This section discusses semantic phenomena that our mapping does and does not capture, providing a lens for assessing the usefulness of the Stanford Dependencies as a semantic resource.

4.1 Successes

Formulas 1-7 are correct HLFs that our mapping rules successfully generate. They illustrate the diversity of semantic information that is easily recoverable from Stanford dependency parses.

Formulas 1-2 show successful parses in simple transitive sentences with active/passive alternations, and Formula 3 demonstrates success in parsing ditransitives. Also easily recovered from the dependency structures are semantic parses of sentences with adverbs (Formula 4) and reporting verbs (Formula 5). Lest it appear that these phenomena may only be handled in isolation, Equations 6-7 show successful parses for sentences with arbitrary combinations of the above phenomena.

A boy builds a boat.
$(\exists e_1, x_1, x_2)[Exist(e_1) \wedge boy(x_2) \wedge boat(x_1) \wedge builds'(e_1, x_2, x_1)]$ (1)

A boat was built by a boy.
$(\exists e_1, x_1, x_2)[Exist(e_1) \wedge boat(x_2) \wedge boy(x_1) \wedge built'(e_1, x_1, x_2)]$ (2)

John gave Mary a boat.
$(\exists e_1, x_1)[Exist(e_1) \wedge boat(x_1) \wedge gave'(e_1, John, x_1, Mary)]$ (3)

John built a boat quickly.
OR ***John quickly built a boat.***
$(\exists e_1, e_2, x_1)[Exist(e_1) \wedge boat(x_1) \wedge quickly(e_2, e_1) \wedge built'(e_1, John, x_1)]$ (4)

John told Mary that a boy built a boat.
$(\exists e_1, e_2, x_1, x_4)[Exist(e_1) \wedge boy(x_1) \wedge boat(x_4) \wedge built'(e_2, x_1, x_4) \wedge told'(e_1, John, Mary, e_2)]$ (5)

John told Mary that Sue told Joe that Adam loves Eve.
$(\exists e_1, e_2, e_3)[Exist(e_1) \wedge told'(e_2, Sue, Joe, e_3) \wedge loves'(e_3, Adam, Eve) \wedge told'(e_1, John, Mary, e_2)]$ (6)

John was told by Mary that Sue wants Joe to build a boat quickly.
$(\exists e_1, e_2, e_3, e_4, x_7)[Exist(e_1) \wedge boat(x_7) \wedge build'(e_2, Joe, x_7) \wedge told'(e_1, Mary, John, e_4) \wedge wants'(e_4, Sue, e_3) \wedge quickly'(e_3, e_2)]$ (7)

4.2 Limitations

Though our mapping rules enable us to directly extract deep semantic information directly from the Stanford dependency parses in the above cases, there are a number of difficulties with this approach that shed light on inherent limitations of the Stanford Dependencies as a semantic resource.

A major such limitation arises in cases of event nominalizations. Because dependency parses are syntax-based, their structures do not distinguish between eventive noun phrases like "the bombing of the city" and non-eventive ones like "the mother of the child"; such a distinction, however, would be found in the corresponding HLFs.

Certain syntactic alternations also prove problematic. For example, the dependency structure does not recognize that "window" takes the same semantic role in the sentences "John broke the mirror." and "The mirror broke." The use of additional semantic resources, like PropBank (Palmer et al., 2005), would be necessary to determine this.

Prepositional phrases present another problem for our mapping task, as the Stanford dependencies will typically not distinguish between PPs indicating arguments and adjuncts. For example, "Mary stuffed envelopes with coupons" and "Mary stuffed envelopes with John" have identical dependency structures, yet "coupons" and "John" are (hopefully for John) taking on different semantic roles. This is, in fact, a prime example of how Stanford dependency parses may resolve syntactic ambiguity without resolving semantic ambiguity.

Of course, one might manage more HLF coverage by adding more rules to our system, but the limitations discussed here are fundamental. If two sentences have different semantic interpretations but identical dependency structures, then there can *be* no deterministic mapping rule (based on dependency structure alone) that yields this distinction.

5 Conclusion

We have presented here our attempt to map the Stanford Dependencies to HLF via a second layer of hand-written rules. That our mapping rules, which are purely a function of dependency structure, succeed in producing correct HLFs in some cases is good evidence that the Stanford Dependencies do contain some practical level of semantic information. Nevertheless, we were also able to quickly identify aspects of meaning that the Stanford Dependencies did not capture.

Our argument does not require that HLF be an optimal representation, only that it capture worthwhile aspects of semantics and that it not be readily derived from the Stanford representation. This is enough to conclude that the Stanford Dependencies are not complete as a meaning representation. While not surprising (as they are intended as a syntactic representation), we hope this short study will help further discussion on what the community wants or needs in a meaning representation: what gaps are acceptable, if any, and whether a more "complete" representation is needed.

Acknowledgments

This material is partially based on research sponsored by the NSF under grant IIS-1249516 and DARPA under agreement number FA8750-13-2-0017 (the DEFT program).

References

Nathanael Chambers, Daniel Cer, Trond Grenager, David Hall, Chloe Kiddon, Bill MacCartney, Marie-Catherine de Marneffe, Daniel Ramage, Eric Yeh, and Christopher D Manning. 2007. Learning alignments and leveraging natural logic. In *Proceedings of the ACL-PASCAL Workshop on Textual Entailment and Paraphrasing*, pages 165–170. Association for Computational Linguistics.

Ido Dagan, Oren Glickman, and Bernardo Magnini. 2005. The pascal recognising textual entailment challenge. In *Proceedings of the PASCAL Challenges Workshop on Recognising Textual Entailment*.

Donald Davidson. 1967. The logical form of action sentences. In *The Logic of Decision and Action*, pages 81–120. Univ. of Pittsburgh Press.

Marie-Catherine De Marneffe, Bill MacCartney, and Christopher D Manning. 2006. Generating typed dependency parses from phrase structure parses. In *Proceedings of LREC*, volume 6, pages 449–454.

Aria D Haghighi, Andrew Y Ng, and Christopher D Manning. 2005. Robust textual inference via graph matching. In *Proceedings of the conference on Human Language Technology and Empirical Methods in Natural Language Processing*, pages 387–394. Association for Computational Linguistics.

Jerry R Hobbs. 1985. Ontological promiscuity. In *Proceedings of the 23rd annual meeting on Association for Computational Linguistics*, pages 60–69. Association for Computational Linguistics.

Dan Klein and Christopher D Manning. 2003. Accurate unlexicalized parsing. In *Proceedings of the 41st Annual Meeting on Association for Computational Linguistics-Volume 1*, pages 423–430. Association for Computational Linguistics.

Bill MacCartney. 2009. *Natural language inference*. Ph.D. thesis, Stanford University.

Martha Palmer, Daniel Gildea, and Paul Kingsbury. 2005. The proposition bank: An annotated corpus of semantic roles. *Computational Linguistics*, 31(1):71–106.

Qualities of Eventiveness

Sean Monahan, Mary Brunson
Language Computer Corporation
{smonahan,mary}@languagecomputer.com

Abstract

Events are not a discrete linguistic phenomenon. Different verbal and nominal predicates express different degrees of eventiveness. In this paper we analyze the qualities that contribute to the overall eventiveness of a predicate, that is, what makes a predicate an event. We provide an in-depth analysis of seven key qualities, along with experimental assessments demonstrating their contributions. We posit that these qualities are an important part of a functional working definition of events.

1 Introduction

The problem of event extraction is fundamentally challenging because many definitions of "event" exist. Some predicates clearly indicate events, e.g. "I *ran* 5 miles to the store", while others indicate states, e.g. "He *is* tall". However, in natural language text, many predicates fall between these two extremes, e.g. "He *runs* frequently". In order to successfully extract events, resolve event coreference across documents, and reason about the events, we must understand exactly what an event is. In this paper, we propose a series of qualities that contribute to the overall *eventiveness* of a predicate. We define eventiveness as "the degree to which a predicate is like an event?".

The concept of "event" is not discrete, but exists along several dimensions. We identify seven qualities of predicates that lead readers to more readily consider them to be events. In order to successfully utilize events in end applications, we believe these qualities must be fully understood.

In this paper, we consider the predicate to be the word (e.g. verb or noun) in the sentence that might indicate the existence of an event. This is also referred to as a *trigger* or *anchor* in event extraction.

Each of the predicates in the following examples (indicated by italics) exhibit different degrees of eventiveness.

1. The tremors have re-awakened bitter memories of the Asian *tsunami* that killed 168,000.
2. Indonesia lies in a zone where the plates shift, sometimes generating *tsunamis*.
3. Electricity was cut off to the city, where people fled their homes fearing a *tsunami*.

The first example is most clearly an event, referring to a specific instance of a tsunami. In the second sentence, the nominal predicate "tsunamis" refers to a non-specific event that occurs as a result a natural occurrence. In the third, a tsunami has not occurred but is a feared possibility.

Any end application of extracted events must decide which of these predicates to consider as relevant. An application to "map known tsunamis" might only consider the first event as relevant. An application to detect newsworthy or "emerging" events might only consider the third. An application seeking to understand relationships between events could utilize the second example to determine that plates shifting causes tsunamis. In order to facilitate a wide range of applications, all of these predicates should be extracted as "events", which can then be separated by the qualities they possess. Furthermore, consideration of these qualities should reflect human judgment about events.

In this paper, we discuss the different qualities that contribute to the eventiveness of a predicate. In Section 2, we describe previous work on defining events. In Section 3, we describe the qualities that we consider to be most representative of events. In Section 4, we describe an experiment we conducted to rate these qualities in terms of how they contribute to eventiveness. In Section 5, we conclude with a summary of our theory of events and a description of how this will aid applications in understanding events.

Proceedings of the 2nd Workshop on EVENTS: Definition, Detection, Coreference, and Representation, pages 59–67,
Baltimore, Maryland, USA, June 22-27, 2014. ©2014 Association for Computational Linguistics

2 Related Work

There have been significant efforts to understand the idea of "events" in a variety of different communities, including physics, philosophy, psychology, and both theoretical and computational linguistics. We draw our qualities of eventiveness from across this literature in order to form a more complete view of what an event is.

Quine (1985) considers an event to be a well-individuated physical object which is clearly defined in space and time. This contrasts with the TimeML schema (Pustejovsky et al., 2003), which regards event as a "a cover term for situations that happen or occur". Lombard (1986) considers an event to necessarily be a change. These definitions by themselves do not sufficiently explain the full boundary between event and non-event, but are useful in informing our qualities.

In addition to TimeML, a pragmatic definition of events was also adopted for ACE (2005). ACE utilized a wide definition of event, though only a small set of event types were annotated, along with their specificity, actuality, and arguments. More recently, TAC KBP (2014) has built on the ACE definition in order to extract event information to incorporate into a knowledge base.

Understanding how events are perceived by individuals has also been researched by psychologists in order to learn how people construct mental models of events. Radvansky and Zacks (2011) investigate the mental representation of an event and how this encompasses the event's spatiotemporal location, the people and objects involved, and the relations between these elements. A working definition of events should consider these psychological conceptions.

The problem of understanding specific events is closely related to that of *event identity*, which considers whether two events mentioned in text are regarded as the same. Many of the definitions of event identity found in literature (e.g. Bejan and Harabagiu, 2010) were established to facilitate event coreference. Hovy et al. (2013) move beyond exact event coreference to consider the notion of *quasi-identity*. Quasi-identity refers to events which are the same in some respects, but not in others. We believe that definitions of events that restrict certain qualities are not effective for informing the quasi-identity relationship. For example, generic events can inform specific instances of that event type.

In the field of theoretical linguistics, there are many concepts that contribute to the idea of eventiveness, including aktionsart and transitivity. Vendler (1957) introduced the classification of verbs into different aspectual (aktionsart) categories, including accomplishments, achievements, activities, and states. The first three categories all correspond with the idea of events, though to varying degrees. In distinguishing between events and states, Comrie (1976) discusses the important factor that states do not require energy to maintain, while events do. Also, Talmy (2000) and Croft (2012) discuss at length the related notion of force-dynamic relations, which deals with the transmission of force between participants.

Additionally, there exists a significant overlap between the dimensions of grammatical transitivity (as a prototypical notion) and the qualities that define events. The concept of transitivity has been researched extensively within the linguistics community, primarily with the goal of understanding grammatical relationships within clauses.

Hopper and Thompson (1980) propose ten different dimensions intended to measure the notion of transitivity, which the authors define as a property of a clause that communicates how effectively an action is "transferred" or "carried-over" from agent to patient. The more effectively the activity can be carried over, the higher the transitivity.

Although Hopper and Thompson suggest that there is no single semantic notion that encompasses the nature of transitivity, they state that they have considered terms such as 'activity' and 'intensity', both of which are also relevant to the notion of eventiveness. Tsunoda (1981; 1985) adds several dimensions to the notion of transitivity as a prototype which we believe further support the relationship between transitivity and eventiveness, including genericity, completion, and realization.

Experimental work was conducted by Madnani et al. (2010) to collect information about subjects' perception of the various transitivity dimensions for given actions. However, the authors do not examine the transitivity dimensions of mode (realis vs. irrealis), agency, and individuation of the object, all of which we regard as also playing a very important part in a predicate's measure of "eventiveness". Additionally, they guide the subjects through the process of measuring transitivity by prompting them for specific properties, as opposed to utilizing human intuition.

Quality	Definition
Occurrence	The quality of a predicate that signals that a change in the state of the world has taken place.
Spatio-Temporal Grounding	The degree to which the predicate is grounded in time and space.
Lexical Aspect	The boundedness and duration of the predicate with respect to time.
Agency	The degree to which the main event participant can be regarded as a "causer" or "doer".
Affectedness	The degree to which the action of the predicate affects the semantic patient.
Actuality	The knowledge of whether the predicate actually took/takes place.
Specificity	The degree to which the predicate refers to a particular instance of an event.

Table 1: Definitions of Event Qualities

3 Qualities of Events

Given the wide array of definitions and descriptions of events from different perspectives, we believe that each offers a unique insight into this multi-faceted problem. We seek to identify the qualities of eventiveness and determine which are the most salient. The seven qualities we consider are listed in Table 1. In this section, we provide a detailed definition, examples, and justification as to why each quality is important to eventiveness. For our examples, we consider predicates with explicit textual indicators of the qualities. However, many predicates can possess these qualities independent of textual evidence. Additionally, although every quality is examined in isolation here, the interaction between these qualities is an important consideration. In Section 4, we describe the experiment we conducted in order to demonstrate the extent to which each quality contributes to eventiveness.

3.1 Occurrence

Occurrence, the idea of something having happened, largely coincides with what we believe to be an event. In fact, the TimeML definition (Pustejovsky et al., 2003) of *event* covers situations that "happen or occur". We consider this to be equivalent to the idea of "change in the state of the world", because if the final state is the same as the initial state, then nothing can be said to have happened or occurred. As such, we contend that the greater the degree to which an event can be considered to have "happened" or "occurred", the greater the amount of eventiveness it will exhibit.

Note that the determination of 'state' here goes beyond mere appearances: a person who bounces a ball and catches it appears to be in exactly the same state as before, but in reality, some energy has been expended. Most verbs exhibit the quality of having "occurred", with the notable exception of statives[1], which are a fairly lexically constrained category (copular verbs, many verbs of cognition, etc.). Thus, for verbal predicates, we can regard verbs that indicate an action rather than a state as having "occurred" and being eventive. In general, the more energy and motion involved in the predicate, the more eventive it is. In the example below, *running* would be considered more eventive than *sitting*.

1. He was *running* on the track. (high energy)
2. He was *sitting* in the chair. (low energy)

For nominal events, the situation is more complicated. We must distinguish the set of nouns that can indicate an event, such as "earthquake", from the set of nouns which cannot, such as "epicenter". For deverbal nouns, we also must distinguish between process nouns, such as "the *building* of the house", and result nouns, as in "the *building* I work in". In order to distinguish the quality of occurrence, we can use the diagnostic of determining whether the predicate can be appropriately associated with words such as "happened", "took place", or "occurred". For example, a *presentation* event can "occur", but the physical materials also called the *presentation* cannot be said to have "occurred".

1. The *presentation* occurred in the boardroom.
2. *The *presentation* slides occurred.

3.2 Spatio-Temporal Grounding

Spatio-temporal grounding deals with the degree to which an event is able to be "pinpointed" to a particular time and place. We hypothesize that a predicate that is more able to be grounded in time and/or space will be perceived as being more eventive than a predicate which is less able to be grounded spatio-temporally.

Quine (1985) considers events to be individuated by their placement in space and time, which implies that any given event should be able to be associated with both a time and a place. Indeed, the close association of events with their locations and times manifests itself in our ability to refer to well-known events by their time or location,

[1] Note that TimeML has a special class of events marked as STATE.

such as *Chernobyl* or *9/11*. Another consequence of the spatio-temporal grounding of events is that one can refer to events that happen relative to other events, e.g. *before*, *after*, *nearby*. Of the following examples, the last seems most eventive.

1. He *fought* the law.
2. He *fought* the law yesterday.
3. He *fought* the law yesterday in court.

3.3 Lexical Aspect

Lexical aspect deals not with *when* a predicate occurs in relation to time (i.e. *tense*), but *how*. It examines, as Comrie (1976) puts it, "the internal temporal constituency of a situation". This covers both how the event is bounded in time (telicity) and how long it lasts (durativity). A durative event can allow for increased eventiveness in that it allows for more changes in the state of the world simply because it lasts longer. At the same time, many punctual (instantaneous) events have the potential to be very eventive because they can produce large amounts of change in a very short time, therefore producing a more *drastic* change (e.g. an assassination or fatal lightning strike). Thus, both durative and non-durative events seem to be able to contribute to eventiveness in unique ways.

Regarding telicity, we believe that events which are bounded in time (i.e. having endpoints) generally evoke a more pronounced sense of eventiveness because they are more easily distinguishable from the "backdrop" of other occurrences and states. In fact, it is by definition that all events must have a beginning (otherwise, they would not be able to be referred to as "occurrences"), and we believe that event endings or markers of completion move an event even closer to a prototypical notion of "high eventiveness".

Vendler (1957) categorizes verbs into four categories depending on their durativity and telicity: *state*, *achievement* (telic, punctual), *accomplishment* (telic, durative), *activity* (atelic, durative). Comrie (1976) adds to this the category of *semelfactive* (atelic, punctual). Examples of these categories follow.

1. He is *building* a house. (telic, durative)
2. He is *swimming*. (atelic, durative)
3. He *shot* the man. (telic, punctual)
4. He is *knocking* on the door. (atelic, punctual)

3.4 Agency

Agency deals with the amount of control and volition involved in an event. We regard agency as a measure of the degree to which a participant willfully executes an action and maintains control over it. As such, we assert that the greater the degree of agency attributed to the causer or performer of an predicate, the higher the eventiveness that the predicate will display. Involved in this idea are the related notions of frequency/normalcy of occurrence and causality. Consider the following.

1. The wine *aged* in a barrel. (no agent)
2. The vintner *aged* the wine in a barrel. (agent: *vintner*)

The presence of the agent causes the second predicate to seem more eventive than the first. The first implies a natural process. The second implies a volitional effort on the part of the vintner (the agent) to cause the wine to undergo this process in a particular location, likely with some control over when the aging would begin and end before being bottled. The relevance of these predicates to many applications is dependent on the existence of the agent.

Dowty (1991) lists prototypical characteristics of high and low agency. For high agency, he lists volition, sentience, effect upon another participant, and self-produced mobility. For low agency, he lists internal change, incremental theme (when something incrementally disappears or is used up), and movement induced by another participant.

We can describe "natural processes" as those occurrences which come about as a result of actions whose main participants are characterized by low agency. Most natural processes, such as "aging", are not considered very eventive. However, distinct from these are certain natural *occurrences* that do involve movement and great effect on the world (such as earthquakes, lightning, and landslides).

We also hypothesize that the frequency or "normalcy" of predicates is related to the degree to which they are perceived as eventive. The growth of grass (low agency) is an extremely frequent and "normal" type of process (and thus should be seen as less eventive), whereas an earthquake (higher agency) is a much rarer occurrence and should therefore be seen as more eventive. Note that this factor is also highly relevant to the "newsworthiness" of the predicate.

Agency is also intricately linked to causality, since prototypical agents often cause a change of state in patients. In many cases, the agent of a particular event can itself be characterized as an event (e.g. "The *earthquake* caused three buildings to crumble"). In this example, the earthquake - while formally the agent of the "crumble" event - is itself considered to be an event.

3.5 Affectedness

Affectedness is the degree to which an event affects its participants, most importantly the participant in the semantic patient role of the predicate. We generally hypothesize that the more affected a patient is by the event it is a participant of, the greater the eventiveness of that predicate.

The actual manifestation of the notion of "affectedness" can take a variety of forms. First, we posit that an event can affect its patient to a greater extent if the patient is more animate. To this end, we consider a general animacy hierarchy that is a modification of the hierarchy proposed by Silverstein (1976): *Human Proper Noun* > *Human Common Noun* > *Animate Noun* > *Inanimate Noun*, e.g. *Sheila* > *woman* > *bear* > *rock.*

Second, we suggest that an event can affect its patient to a greater extent if the action that is taking place is more severe or extreme. For example, we would consider "He *killed* the man" to be more eventive than "He *wounded* the man", simply because of the longer-lasting effect of "kill".

Both of these notions are grounded in Hopper and Thompson's (1980) transitivity dimensions of *Individuation of O* and *Affectedness of O*, where O generally represents the semantic patient. They contend that a particular action is able to be "more effectively transferred" to a highly individuated patient (one that is a proper noun, human or animate, concrete, singular, count, and referential/definite) than to a patient that is low in individuation (one that is common, inanimate, abstract, plural, mass, and non-referential). We believe that eventiveness has a direct correlation with patient individuation in all dimensions but one: the singular vs. plural distinction. We contend that all other things being equal, the broader the semantic patient role is, the greater the overall effect of the event (e.g. *He killed five men* as opposed to *He killed one man*), and therefore the greater the eventiveness.

1. He *punched* some pillows. (low individuation)
2. He *punched* his brother. (high individuation)
3. He *bruised* the man's leg. (low affectedness)
4. He *broke* the man's leg. (high affectedness)

Tsunoda (1981) notes that this affectedness is independent of the amount of agency the agent possesses: a person killed by a stray bullet is just as affected as a person who is intentionally killed.

Our experiment in this study tests primarily for individuation, and further testing is required to specifically examine Hopper and Thompson's *affectedness of O* dimension. Additionally, future studies could examine Tsunoda's (1981) claim that resultative predicates (e.g. *break, kill*) generally encode higher transitivity than non-resultative predicates (e.g. *hit, shoot*). We believe that such predicates should exhibit higher eventiveness because they lexically explicate the change in the world that has taken place as a result of an action. Similarly, future experiments could consider not only the patient, but also how the agent and/or other participants are affected by the action.

3.6 Specificity

Specificity can be defined as the degree to which a predicate refers to a particular instance (or instances) of an event, where that event must be well-grounded in time and space and well-individuated from other events. We believe that as specificity of a predicate increases, eventiveness increases as well. Thus, specific events should have higher eventiveness than habitual events (ones that recur but do not have a well-defined spatio-temporal location and/or number of occurrences), and generic events (where no specific instance is in focus).

While both habitual and generic predicates are less eventive, they differ in several ways. Habitual events typically imply that instances of the event have occurred, but with no specific information about these occurrences, whereas generic predicates refer to events that are treated more as general classes of occurrences in the world rather than individuated events. The following examples illustrate this quality.

1. The chicken laid an egg on Tuesday. (specific)
2. The chicken lays two eggs a week. (habitual)
3. Chickens lay eggs when fertile. (generic)

As noted in the example in the introduction, habitual and generic events are of great value for acquiring world knowledge that can apply to specific instances of those events. We consider this task to be very similar to detecting when two events share quasi-identity (Hovy et al., 2013). In the above example, the habitual event gives a likely next date for egg laying, and the generic event gives us the knowledge that the chicken is fertile and therefore able to lay eggs.

We also hypothesize that the more specific the event (e.g. *lays an egg on Tuesdays and Fridays* rather than *lays two eggs a week*), the more eventive the predicate will seem. This intuition connects with recent research into detecting the difference between habitual and specific events (Mathew and Katz, 2009), where the existence of semantic arguments to the predicate contributes to specificity. Often, arguments missing from generic events would display other properties of eventiveness (e.g., agency or spatio-temporal grounding) if they were present.

3.7 Actuality

Actuality refers to whether an action is realis or irrealis, that is, whether or not it actually occurs. We regard actualized (realis) predicates as exhibiting a higher eventiveness than unactualized (irrealis) predicates, as the former present actual changes in the state of the world, whereas the latter posit only potential or hypothetical changes.

The notion of whether or not a predicate is actualized corresponds to the "Effectiveness Condition" parameter of *realization* (Tsunoda, 1981) in transitivity theory. A predicate's fulfillment of the Effectiveness Condition generally correlates to a greater "completeness" of lexical meaning and also corresponds to a higher degree of affectedness of the patient.

There are a wide variety of contexts in which irrealis predicates can occur; among these, predicates may be modified by epistemic modality (*might have*), deontic modality (*hopes, orders, promises*), abilities (*is able to*), and negative polarity (*didn't*). We also consider future tense events to be irrealis, as by definition they have not yet occurred. It should be noted that epistemic events exist between realis and irrealis, and may exhibit more eventiveness than other forms of modality.

Within the class of negative events, we can contrast simple negation events (events modified by negators such as *no* and *not*) with avoided or prevented events. Avoided events involve a conscious decision (thus requiring agency) to not perpetrate the event. Prevented events, on the other hand, involve an external agent preventing the event from occurring. In general, the act of preventing an event from occurring is itself an event.

1. He *bought* a new car. (realis)
2. He might *buy* a new car. (future)
3. He might have *bought* a new car. (epistemic)
4. He is able to *buy* a new car. (ability)
5. He wants to *buy* a new car. (deontic)
6. He was prevented from *buying* a new car. (negative, prevention)
7. He did not *buy* a new car. (negative, simple negation)

Typically, systems which utilize events concentrate on realis events only; however, when dealing with events across documents, the information associated with irrealis predicates is very useful for establishing quasi-identity relationships. There are several motivating examples of unactualized event types that are necessary for deeper understanding of events. If a crime occurs, for instance, a particular suspect's *ability* to commit that crime becomes relevant. Likewise, if some order is given to perform an action, and the action later occurs, the quasi-identity relationship between the "director" and the action is immediately relevant.

4 Experiment

In order to perform a concrete analysis of the qualities of eventiveness in the real world, we undertook a small experiment in which human participants rated the eventiveness of different predicates in context. We hypothesize that a predicate with an explicit indicator of one of these qualities would be considered more eventive than a similar predicate without that indicator.

4.1 Methodology

For each quality, we created one sentence with and one without explicit evidence of that quality. The two sentences utilize the same predicate and differ only in their expression of the quality of interest. For example, "He *graduated* college" possesses the positive actuality quality, while "He promised to *graduate* college" does not. This allows us to compare the ratings for these pairs of sentences.

The sentences were placed into example groups consisting of a pseudo-random sampling of the sentences, enforced to only have one instance of a predicate within each group. Each example group

Mechanical Turk Instructions
Directions: Please rate the following words in terms of whether they indicate an event in the context of the given sentence located above each word. A rating of '5' means that it is very much an event, and a '1' rating means that it is not at all an event. Read the definition/examples below carefully before beginning.
Definition: An event is a cover term for situations that happen or occur. Events can be punctual (instantaneous) or last for a period of time.
Examples: 1. I am **building** a new house. (*building* is an event) 2. I like the Empire State **Building**. (*Building* is not an event, but an object) 3. Robert **grew** to be tall. (*grew* is an event) 4. Robert **is** tall. (*is* is not an event)
Question Prompt: How much like an event does this word seem? **1** (not at all) **2** (slightly) **3** (moderately) **4** (fairly) **5** (very)

Table 2: Annotation Instructions

consisted of eight example sentences, with a total of nine example groups.

We collected the eventiveness ratings from participants on Amazon Mechanical Turk, who rated each predicate in the example group on an integer scale from one to five. We collected 50 ratings for each sentence, and participants were allowed to complete multiple example groups. Overall, we had 76 unique participants, who completed an average of 5.9 example groups each. The participants spent an average of 9 seconds rating the predicate in each sentence.

We also included a variety of control "non-events", which included result nouns as well as statives. These exhibited statistically lower eventiveness than any of the non-control predicates.

4.1.1 Instructions

We provided instructions to each participant as shown in Table 2. These instructions contain a succinct definition of an event, utilizing the TimeML terminology (Pustejovsky et al., 2003). Additionally, we provided four example sentences, two illustrating events and two illustrating non-events. One of the non-events was a stative ("is"), and the other was a result noun ("Building"). These examples illustrate that not all verbs indicate events, and that words like "building" can be events in some contexts but not others.

4.2 Analysis

For our analysis, we examined the mean, variance, and ranking of the eventiveness ratings provided for each predicate by the participants. We compared pairs of sentences[2] based on the probability that a randomly chosen rating for the sentence with the quality would be higher than a randomly chosen rating for the sentence without the quality. The statistical significance of this probability can be assessed using a Wilcoxin-Mann-Whitney test.

For example, "He *played* piano" has a mean eventiveness rating of $\overline{x}$=4.56, σ=.80, and "He is able to *play* piano" has $\overline{x}$=3.82, σ=1.35. A random rating for *played* is 66.3% more likely to be higher than one for the ability *play*. This difference is statistically significant assuming an acceptable type-I error rate of .05%.

We present in Table 3 results for the pairs of sentences testing each quality with their probabilities. The > indicates the hypothesis that one value of the quality is more eventive than the other. The * indicates statistical significance.

Quality	Result	Prob
Occurrence	Verb > Noun	0.604*
Occurrence	High Energy > Low Energy	0.686*
Spatial	Grounded > Not	0.526
Temporal	Grounded > Not	0.509
Agency	Agency > No Agency	0.641*
Aspect	Atelic Durative > Telic Punctual	0.628*
Aspect	Telic Durative > Atelic Durative	0.471
Affectedness	Individuated > Not	0.505
Actuality	Actual > Ability	0.663*
Actuality	Actual > Epistemic Modality	0.646*
Actuality	Actual > Volitive Modality	0.664*
Actuality	Actual > Commissive Modality	0.620*
Actuality	Actual > Directive Modality	0.642*
Actuality	Actual > Polarity	0.681*
Actuality	Past Tense > Future	0.635*
Actuality	Present Tense > Future	0.626*
Specificity	Specific > Habitual	0.667*
Specificity	Specific > Generic	0.546

Table 3: Results of Eventiveness for Qualities

4.3 Discussion of Results

As shown in Table 3, many of the factors that have been identified in various theoretical descriptions of eventiveness can be shown experimentally to affect people's perception of the eventiveness of a predicate in a sentence. Below, we discuss the positive results, where our hypotheses were confirmed, as well as the negative results.

[2]A complete list is available by request.

For occurrence, agency, and actuality, we found strong evidence that these qualities contribute to eventiveness. For example, "The *attack* happened at dawn" was less eventive than "They *attacked* at dawn", "The fire *started*" was less eventive than "He *started* the fire", and "He hopes to *graduate college*" was less eventive than "He *graduated* college". For actuality, realis predicates were always more eventive than irrealis predicates. An ANOVA test indicated no significant difference between the different forms of irrealis (modality, negation, etc.).

Results for the other qualities were slightly more mixed. For aspect, we found that activities were more eventive than achievements, but contrary to expectation, accomplishments were not more eventive than activities. For specificity, there was a clear distinction between specific and habitual predicates, but no distinction between specific and generic predicates. Our example of a generic predicate, "Football fans watch the Superbowl" could be considered either a generic event or a present tense description, and this might have confused the results. Also, since the definition provided for *event* gave only singular event examples, this may have biased the results in this case.

For spatio-temporal grounding, there was no significant effect. We believe that this is due to the implicit eventive nature of some verbs. We analyzed the predicate "fought", which was equally eventive with and without a specified time or location. However, such a verb does not require explicit grounding; the reader can assume that any given fight happens at a specific time and location. For affectedness, our examples utilized a verb that is always highly indicative of affectedness and did not adequately capture a good distinction between high and low affectedness. We believe that future experiments can control for these kinds of cases and that example predicates can be found that will isolate the specific qualities.

Another concern is that our design only explicitly tested a single predicate for each quality. However, the nature of the predicates and the sentences we used allowed for post-hoc analysis of the qualities that existed across more than two sentences. Empirical testing showed the same pattern of results across predicates for these qualities.

Overall, the experimental results are extremely interesting in their congruence with the literature on events, but further research is required to determine the exact contribution of each quality. The current experimental design lacks sufficient power to reliably rank the qualities due to contrast effects within example groups. It is likely that the ordering/grouping of the examples affected the rating of individual examples. In future studies, we plan to control for these effects by controlling the ordering of the examples given to each individual.

5 Conclusion

Working definitions of events are often ill-defined and difficult to apply. We have laid out a series of qualities which contribute to the overall eventiveness of a predicate in a sentence. Our findings indicate that the degree to which a predicate is considered an event is a function of these qualities. Evidence for these qualities was validated using participant ratings of predicates.

When developing annotated corpora of events, the decision of whether or not to consider an individual predicate as an event is difficult. Understanding the qualities of eventiveness can explain why one predicate seems less eventive than another (e.g. irrealis, generic).

Instead of deciding each predicate on the basis of the individual qualities being exhibited, annotation specifications should consider how these qualities interact. Drawing an explicit boundary between events and non-events can cause information contained in the non-events to be lost for reasoning. Along the same lines, event extraction capabilities could be greatly improved by the labelling of these qualities on annotated corpora. This would enable event extraction to preserve the fine-grained distinctions between events that are shown to be relevant to human understanding.

In this study, we gave examples of how predicates with lesser eventiveness can provide valuable insight into problems such as event coreference and quasi-identity resolution. These qualities of eventiveness can serve to inform future research into those areas, providing a deeper understanding of the meaning of event coreference. While different applications have different needs, understanding the qualities that contribute to eventiveness will enable applications to more intelligently utilize event information.

6 Acknowledgements

This work was sponsored in part by the Air Force Research Laboratory (AFRL).

References

ACE. 2005. In *ACE (Automatic Content Extraction) English Annotation Guidelines for Events Version 5.4.3 2005.07.01*.

Cosmin Bejan and Sanda Harabagiu. 2010. Unsupervised event coreference resolution with rich linguistic features. In *Proceedings of the 48th Annual Meeting of the Association for Computational Linguistics*, pages 1412–1422, Uppsala, Sweden, July. Association for Computational Linguistics.

Bernard Comrie. 1976. Aspect: An introduction to the study of verbal aspect and related problems. Cambridge University Press.

William Croft. 2012. In *Verbs: Aspect and Causal Structure*, Oxford. Oxford University Press.

David Dowty. 1991. Thematic proto-roles and argument selection. In *Language, Vol. 67, No. 3.*, pages 547–619, September.

Paul J. Hopper and Sandra A. Thompson. 1980. Transitivity in grammar and discourse. In *Language 56 (2)*, pages 251–299, June.

Eduard Hovy, Teruko Mitamura, Felisa Verdejo, Jun Araki, and Andrew Philpot. 2013. Events are not simple: Identity, non-identity, and quasi-identity. In *Proceedings of the NAACL HLT 2013*.

TAC KBP. 2014.
http://www.nist.gov/tac/2014/kbp/event/.

Lawrence B. Lombard. 1986. In *Events: A Metaphysical Study*, London. Routledge and Kegan Paul.

Nitin Madnani, Jordan Boyd-Graber, and Philip Resnik. 2010. Measuring transitivity using untrained annotators. In *Creating Speech and Language Data With Amazon's Mechanical Turk*, Los Angeles, CA.

Thomas A. Mathew and E. Graham Katz. 2009. Supervised categorization of habitual versus episodic sentences. Dissertation. Georgetown University.

James Pustejovsky, Jose Castano, Bob Ingria, Roser Sauri, Rob Gaizauskas, Andrea Setzer, and Graham Katz. 2003. Timeml: Robust specification of event and temporal expressions in text. In *Proceedings of the Fifth International Workshop on Computational Semantics (IWCS)*.

W. V. O. Quine. 1985. Events and reification. In *E. LePore and B. P. McLaughlin, eds., Actions and Events: Perspectives on the philosophy of Donald Davidson*, pages 162–171, Oxford: Blackwell.

Gabriel A. Radvansky and Jeffrey M. Zacks. 2011. Event perception. pages 608–620.

Michael Silverstein. 1976. Hierarchy of features and ergativity. In *Grammatical Categories in Australian Languages*, pages 112–171, Canberra. Australian Institute of Aboriginal Studies.

Leonard Talmy. 2000. Force dynamics in language and cognition. In *Toward a Cognitive Semantics - Vol. 1*, Cambridge, Mass. The MIT Press.

Tasaku Tsunoda. 1981. Split case-marking patterns in verb-types and tense/aspect/mood. In *Linguistics 19, no. 5-6*, pages 389–438.

Tasaku Tsunoda. 1985. Remarks on transitivity. In *Journal of Linguistics 21*, pages 385–396.

Zeno Vendler. 1957. Verbs and times. In *The Philosophical Review. Vol. 66 No. 2*, pages 143–160, April.

Evaluation for Partial Event Coreference

Jun Araki Eduard Hovy Teruko Mitamura
Language Technologies Institute
Carnegie Mellon University
Pittsburgh, PA 15213, USA
junaraki@cs.cmu.edu, hovy@cmu.edu, teruko@cs.cmu.edu

Abstract

This paper proposes an evaluation scheme to measure the performance of a system that detects hierarchical event structure for event coreference resolution. We show that each system output is represented as a forest of unordered trees, and introduce the notion of conceptual event hierarchy to simplify the evaluation process. We enumerate the desiderata for a similarity metric to measure the system performance. We examine three metrics along with the desiderata, and show that metrics extended from MUC and BLANC are more adequate than a metric based on Simple Tree Matching.

1 Introduction

Event coreference resolution is the task to determine whether two event mentions refer to the same event. This task is important since resolved event coreference is useful in various tasks such as topic detection and tracking, information extraction, question answering, textual entailment, and contradiction detection.

A key challenge for event coreference resolution is that one can define several relations between two events, where some of them exhibit subtle deviation from perfect event identity. For clarification, we refer to perfect event identity as *full (event) coreference* in this paper. To address the subtlety in event identity, Hovy et al. (2013) focused on two types of partial event identity: *subevent* and *membership*. Subevent relations form a stereotypical sequence of events, or a script (Schank and Abelson, 1977; Chambers and Jurafsky, 2008). Membership relations represent instances of an event collection. We refer to both as *partial (event) coreference* in this paper. Figure 1 shows some examples of the subevent and membership relations in the illustrative text below, taken from the Intelligence Community domain of violent events. Unlike full coreference, partial coreference is a directed relation, and forms hierarchical event structure, as shown in Figure 1. Detecting partial coreference itself is an important task because the resulting event structures are beneficial to text comprehension. In addition, such structures are also useful as background knowledge information to resolve event coreference.

A car bomb that police said was set by Shining Path guerrillas **ripped off**(E4) the front of a Lima police station before dawn Thursday, **wounding**(E5) 25 people. The **attack**(E6) marked the return to the spotlight of the feared Maoist group, recently overshadowed by a smaller rival band of rebels. The pre-dawn **bombing**(E7) **destroyed**(E8) part of the police station and a municipal office in Lima's industrial suburb of Ate-Vitarte, **wounding**(E9) 8 police officers, one seriously, Interior Minister Cesar Saucedo told reporters. The bomb **collapsed**(E11) the roof of a neighboring hospital, **injuring**(E12) 15, and **blew out**(E13) windows and doors in a public market, **wounding**(E14) two guards.

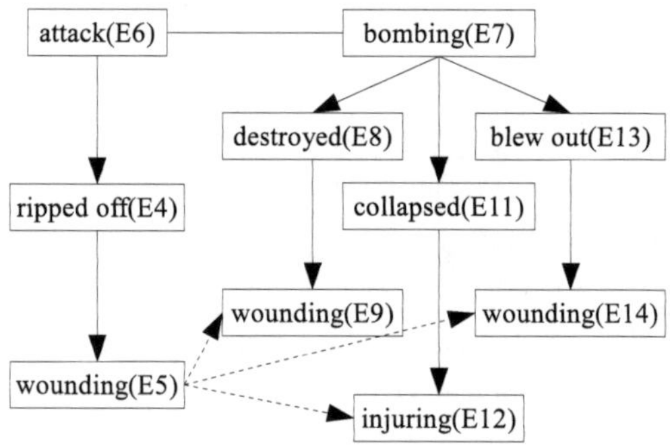

Figure 1: Examples of subevent and membership relations. Solid and dashed arrows represent subevent and membership relations respectively, with the direction from a parent to its subevent or member. For example, we say that E4 is a subevent of E6. Solid lines without any arrow heads represent full coreference.

In this paper, we address the problem of evalu-

Proceedings of the 2nd Workshop on EVENTS: Definition, Detection, Coreference, and Representation, pages 68–76,
Baltimore, Maryland, USA, June 22-27, 2014.

ating the performance of a system that detects partial coreference in the context of event coreference resolution. This problem is important because, as with other tasks, a good evaluation method for partial coreference will facilitate future research on the task in a consistent and comparable manner. When one introduces a certain evaluation metric to such a new complex task as partial event coreference, it is often unclear what metric is suitable to what evaluation scheme for the task under what assumptions. It is also obscure how effectively and readily existing algorithms or tools, if any, can be used in a practical setting of the evaluation. In order to resolve these sub-problems for partial coreference evaluation, we need to formulate an evaluation scheme that defines assumptions to be made regarding the evaluation, specifies some desiderata that an ideal metric should satisfy for the task, and examines how adequately particular metrics can satisfy them. For this purpose, we specifically investigate three existing algorithms MUC, BLANC, and Simple Tree Matching (STM).

The contributions of this work are as follows:

- We introduce a conceptual tree hierarchy that simplifies the evaluation process for partial event coreference.
- We present a way to extend MUC, BLANC, and STM for the case of unordered trees. Those metrics are generic and flexible enough to be used in evaluations involving data structures based on unordered trees.
- Our experimental results indicate that the extended MUC and BLANC are better than Simple Tree Matching for evaluating partial coreference.

2 Related Work

Recent studies on both entity and event coreference resolution use several metrics to evaluate system performance (Bejan and Harabagiu, 2010; Lee et al., 2012; Durrett et al., 2013; Lassalle and Denis, 2013) since there is no agreement on a single metric. Currently, five metrics are widely used: MUC (Vilain et al., 1995), B-CUBED (Bagga and Baldwin, 1998), two CEAF metrics CEAF-ϕ_3 and CEAF-ϕ_4 (Luo, 2005), and BLANC (Recasens and Hovy, 2011). We can divide these metrics into two groups: cluster-based metrics, e.g., B-CUBED and CEAF, and link-based metrics, e.g., MUC and BLANC. The former group is not applicable to evaluate partial coreference because it is unclear how to define a cluster. The latter is not readily applicable to the evaluation because it is unclear how to penalize incorrect directions of links. We discuss these aspects in Section 4.1 and Section 4.2.

Tree Edit Distance (TED) is one of the traditional algorithms for measuring tree similarity. It has a long history of theoretical studies (Tai, 1979; Zhang and Shasha, 1989; Klein, 1998; Bille, 2005; Demaine et al., 2009; Pawlik and Augsten, 2011). It is also widely studied in many applications, including Natural Language Processing (NLP) tasks (Mehdad, 2009; Wang and Manning, 2010; Heilman and Smith, 2010; Yao et al., 2013). However, TED has a disadvantage: we need to predefine appropriate costs for basic tree-edit operations. In addition, an implementation of TED for unordered trees is fairly complex.

Another tree similarity metric is Simple Tree Matching (STM) (Yang, 1991). STM measures the similarity of two trees by counting the maximum match with dynamic programming. Although this algorithm was also originally developed for ordered trees, the underlying idea of the algorithm is simple, making it relatively easy to extend the algorithm for unordered trees.

Tree kernels have been also widely studied and applied to NLP tasks, more specifically, to capture the similarity between parse trees (Collins and Duffy, 2001; Moschitti et al., 2008) or between dependency trees (Croce et al., 2011; Srivastava et al., 2013). This method is based on a supervised learning model with training data; hence we need a number of pairs of trees and associated numeric similarity values between these trees as input. Thus, it is not appropriate for an evaluation setting.

3 Evaluation Scheme

When one formulates an evaluation scheme for a new task, it is important to define assumptions for the evaluation and desiderata that an ideal metric should satisfy. In this section, we first describe assumptions for partial coreference evaluation, and introduce the notion of conceptual event hierarchy to address the challenge posed by one of the assumptions. We then enumerate the desiderata for a metric.

3.1 Assumptions on Partial Coreference

We make the following three assumptions to evaluate partial coreference.

Twinless mentions: Twinless mentions (Stoyanov et al., 2009) are the mentions that exist in the gold standard but do not in a system response, or vice versa. In reality, twinless mentions often happen since an end-to-end system might produce them in the process of detecting mentions. The assumption regarding twinless mentions has been investigated in research on entity coreference resolution. Cluster-based metrics such as B-CUBED and CEAF assume that a system is given true mentions without any twinless mentions in the gold standard, and then resolves full coreference on them. Researchers have made different assumptions about this issue. Early work such as (Ji et al., 2005) and (Bengtson and Roth, 2008) simply ignored such mentions. Rahman and Ng (2009) removed twinless mentions that are singletons in a system response. Cai and Strube (2010) proposed two variants of B-CUBED and CEAF that can deal with twinless mentions in order to make the evaluation of end-to-end coreference resolution system consistent.

In evaluation of partial coreference where twinless mentions can also exist, we believe that the value of making evaluation consistent and comparable is the most important, and hypothesize that it is possible to effectively create a metric to measure the performance of partial coreference while dealing with twinless mentions. A potential problem of making a single metric handle twinless mentions is that the metric would not be informative enough to show whether a system is good at identifying coreference links but poor at identifying mentions, or vice versa (Recasens and Hovy, 2011). However, our intuition is that the problem is avoidable by showing the performance of mention identification with metrics such as precision, recall, and the F-measure simultaneously with the performance of link identification. In this work, therefore, we assume that a metric for partial coreference should be able to handle twinless mentions.

Intransitivity: As described earlier, partial coreference is a directed relation. We assume that partial coreference is not transitive. To illustrate the intransitivity, let $e_i \stackrel{s}{\rightarrow} e_j$ denote a subevent relation that e_j is a subevent of e_i. In Figure 1, we have $E7 \stackrel{s}{\rightarrow} E8$ and $E8 \stackrel{s}{\rightarrow} E9$. In this case, E9 is not a subevent of E7 due to the intransitivity of subevent relations. One could argue that the event 'wounding(E9)' is one of stereotypical events triggered by the event 'bombing(E7)', and thus $E7 \stackrel{s}{\rightarrow} E9$. However, if we allow transitivity of partial coreference, then we have to measure all implicit partial coreference links (e.g., the one between E7 and E9) from hierarchical event structures. Consequently, this evaluation policy could result in an unfair scoring scheme biased toward large event hierarchy.

Link propagation: We assume that partial coreference links can be propagated due to a combination of full coreference links with them. To illustrate the phenomenon, let $e_i \Leftrightarrow e_j$ denote full coreference between e_i and e_j. In Figure 1, we have $E6 \Leftrightarrow E7$ and $E7 \stackrel{s}{\rightarrow} E8$. In this case, E8 is also a subevent of E6, i.e., $E6 \stackrel{s}{\rightarrow} E8$. The rationale behind this assumption is that if a system identifies $E6 \stackrel{s}{\rightarrow} E8$ instead of $E7 \stackrel{s}{\rightarrow} E8$, then there is no reason to argue that the identified subevent relation is incorrect given that $E6 \Leftrightarrow E7$ and $E7 \stackrel{s}{\rightarrow} E8$. The discussion here also applies to membership relations.

3.2 Conceptual Event Hierarchy

The assumption of link propagation poses a challenge in measuring the performance of partial coreference. We illustrate the challenge with the example in the discussion on link propagation above. We focus only on subevent relations to describe our idea, but one can apply the same discussion to membership relations. Suppose that a system detects a subevent link $E7 \stackrel{s}{\rightarrow} E8$, but not $E6 \stackrel{s}{\rightarrow} E8$. Then, is it reasonable to give the system a double reward for two links $E7 \stackrel{s}{\rightarrow} E8$ and $E6 \stackrel{s}{\rightarrow} E8$ due to link propagation, or should one require a system to perform such link propagation and detect $E7 \stackrel{s}{\rightarrow} E8$ as well for the system to achieve the double reward? In the evaluation scheme based on event trees whose nodes represent event mentions, we need to predefine how to deal with link propagation of full and partial coreference in evaluation. In particular, we must pay attention to the potential risk of overcounting partial corefrence links due to link propagation.

To address the complexity of link propagation, we introduce a conceptual event tree where each node represents a conceptual event rather than an event mention. Figure 2 shows an example of a conceptual subevent tree constructed from full coreference and subevent relations in Figure 1. Using set notation, each node of the tree represents an abstract event. For instance, node {E6, E7} represents an "attacking" event which both event mentions E6 and E7 refer to.

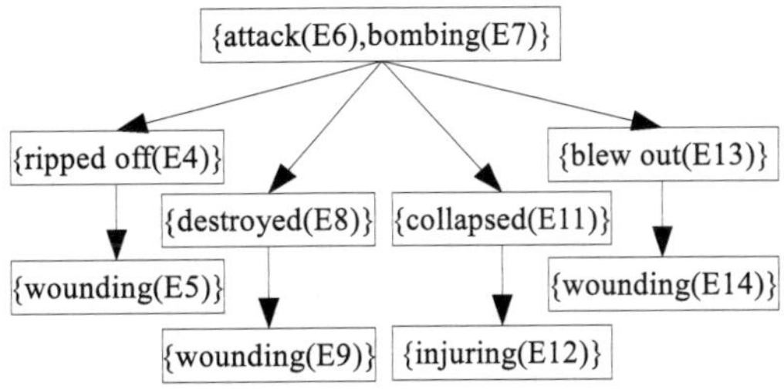

Figure 2: A conceptual subevent tree constructed from the full coreference and subevent relations in Figure 1.

The notion of a conceptual event tree obviates the need to cope with link propagation, thereby simplifying the evaluation for partial coreference. Given a conceptual event tree, an evaluation metric is basically just required to measure how many links in the tree a system successfully detects. When comparing two conceptual event trees, a link in a tree is identical to one in the other tree if there is at least one event mention shared in parent nodes of those links and at least one shared in child nodes of those links. For example, suppose that system A identifies $E6 \xrightarrow{s} E8$, system B $E7 \xrightarrow{s} E8$, system C both, and all the systems identify $E6 \Leftrightarrow E7$ in Figure 1. In this case, they gain the same score since the subevent links that they identify correspond to one correct subevent link $\{E6, E7\} \xrightarrow{s} \{E8\}$ in Figure 2. It is possible to construct the conceptual event hierarchy for membership relations in the same way as described above. This means that the conceptual event hierarchy allows us to show the performance of a system on each type of partial coreference separately, which leads to more informative evaluation output.

One additional note is that the conceptual event tree representing partial coreference is an unordered tree, as illustrated in Figure 2. Although we could represent a subevent tree with an ordered tree because of the stereotypical sequence of subevents given by definition, partial coreference is in general represented with a forest of unordered trees[1].

3.3 Desiderata for Metrics

In general, a system output of partial event coreference in a document is represented not by a single tree but by a forest, i.e., a set of disjoint trees whose nodes are event mentions that appear in the document. Let T be a tree, and let F be a forest $F = \{T_i\}$. Let $sim(F_g, F_r) \in [0, 1]$ denote a similarity score between the gold standard forest F_g and a system response forest F_r. We define the following properties that an ideal evaluation metric for partial event coreference should satisfy.

P1. *Identity*: $sim(F_1, F_1) = 1$.
P2. *Symmetricity*: $sim(F_1, F_2) = sim(F_2, F_1)$.
P3. *Zero*: $sim(F_1, F_2) = 0$ if F_1 and F_2 are totally different forests.
P4. *Monotonicity*: The metric score should increase from 0 to 1 monotonically as two totally different forests approach the identical one.
P5. *Linearity*: The metric score should increase linearly as each single individual correct piece of information is added to a system response.

The first three properties are relatively intuitive. P4 is important because otherwise a higher score by the metric does not necessarily mean higher quality of partial event coreference output. In P5, a correct piece of information is the addition of one correct link or the deletion of one incorrect link. This property is useful for tracking performance progress over a certain period of time. If the metric score increases nonlinearly, then it is difficult to compare performance progress such as a 0.1 gain last year and a 0.1 gain this year, for example.

In addition, one can think of another property with respect to structural consistency. The motivation for the property is that one might want to give more reward to partial coreference links that form hierarchical structures, since they implicitly form sibling relations among child nodes. For instance, suppose that system A detects two links $\{E6, E7\} \xrightarrow{s} \{E8\}$ and $\{E6, E7\} \xrightarrow{s} \{E11\}$, and system B two links $\{E8\} \xrightarrow{s} \{E9\}$ and $\{E11\} \xrightarrow{s} \{E12\}$ in Figure 2. We can think that system A performs better since the system successfully detects an implicit subevent sibling relation between $\{E8\}$ and $\{E11\}$ as well. Due to space limitations, however, we do not explore the property in this work, and leave it for future work.

[1]For example, it is impossible to intuitively define a sequence of child nodes in a membership event tree in Figure 1.

4 Evaluation Metrics

In this section, we examine three evaluation metrics based on MUC, BLANC, and STM respectively under the evaluation scheme described in Section 3.

4.1 B-CUBED and CEAF

B-CUBED regards a coreference chain as a set of mentions, and examines the presence and absence of mentions in a system response that are relative to each of their corresponding mentions in the gold standard (Bagga and Baldwin, 1998). Let us call such set a mention cluster. A problem in applying B-CUBED to partial coreference is that it is difficult to properly form a mention cluster for partial coreference. In Figure 2, for example, we could form a gold standard cluster containing all nodes in the tree. We could then form a system response cluster, given a certain system output. The problem is that B-CUBED's way of counting mentions overlapped in those clusters cannot capture parent-child relations between the mentions in a cluster. It is also difficult to extend the counting algorithm to incorporate such relations in an intuitive manner. Therefore, we observe that B-CUBED is not appropriate for evaluating partial coreference.

We see the basically same reason for the inadequacy of CEAF. It also regards a coreference chain as a set of mentions, and measures how many mentions two clusters share using two similarity metrics $\phi_3(R, S) = |R \cap S|$ and $\phi_4(R, S) = \frac{2|R \cap S|}{|R|+|S|}$, given two clusters R and S. One can extend CEAF for partial coreference by selecting the most appropriate tree similarity algorithm for ϕ that works well with the algorithm to compute maximum bipartite matching in CEAF. However, that is another line of work, and due to space limitations we leave it for future work.

4.2 Extension to MUC and BLANC

MUC relies on the minimum number of links needed when mapping a system response to the gold standard (Vilain et al., 1995). Given a set of key entities K and a set of response entities R, precision of MUC is defined as the number of common links between entities in K and R divided by the number of links in R, whereas recall of MUC is defined as the number of common links between entities in K and R divided by the number of links in K. After finding a set of mention clusters by resolving full coreference, we can compute the number of correct links by counting all links spanning in those mention clusters that matched the gold standard. It is possible to apply the idea of MUC to the case of partial coreference simply by changing the definition of a correct link. In the partial coreference case, we define a correct link as a link matched with the gold standard including its direction. Let MUC_p denote such extension to MUC for partial coreference.

Similarly, it is also possible to define an extension to BLANC. Let BLANC_p denote the extension. BLANC computes precision, recall, and F1 scores for both coreference and non-coreference links, and average them for the final score (Recasens and Hovy, 2011). As with MUC_p, BLANC_p defines a correct link as a link matched with the gold standard including its direction. Another difference between BLANC and BLANC_p is the total number of mention pairs, denoted as L. In the original BLANC, $L = N(N-1)/2$ where N is the total number of mentions in a document. We use $L_p = N(N-1)$ instead for BLANC_p since we consider two directed links in partial coreference with respect to each undirected link in full coreference.

4.3 Extension to Simple Tree Matching

The underlying idea of STM is that if two trees have more node-matching, then they are more similar. The original STM uses a dynamic programming approach to perform recursive node-level matching in a top-down fashion. In the case of partial coreference, we cannot readily use the approach because partial coreference is represented with unordered trees, and thus time complexity of node-matching is the exponential order with respect to the number of child nodes. However, partial event coreference is normally given in a small hierarchy with three levels or less. Taking advantage of this fact and assuming that each event mention is uniquely identified in a tree, we extend STM for the case of unordered trees by using greedy search. Algorithm 1 shows an extension to the STM algorithm for unordered trees.

We can also naturally extend STM to take forests as input. Figure 3 shows how one can convert a forest into a single tree whose subtrees are the trees in the forest by introducing an additional dummy root node on top of those tree. The resulting tree is also an unordered tree, and thus we can apply Algorithm 1 to that tree to measure the sim-

Algorithm 1 Extended simple tree matching for unordered trees.

```
Input: two unordered trees A and B
Output: score
procedure SimpleTreeMatching(A, B)
    if the roots of A and B have different elements then
        return 0
    else
        s := 1                ▷ The initial score for the root match.
        m := the number of first-level sub-trees of A
        n := the number of first-level sub-trees of B
        for i = 1 → m do
            for j = 1 → n do
                if A_i and B_j have the same element then
                    s = s + SimpleTreeMatching(A_i, B_j)
```

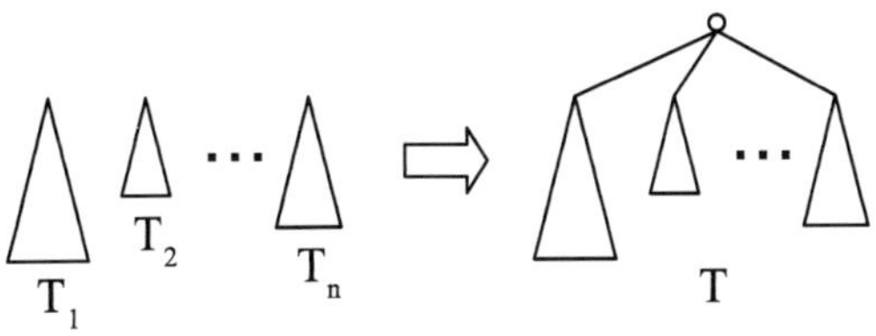

Figure 3: Conversion from a forest to a single tree with an additional dummy root.

ilarity of two forests comprising unordered trees. Let STM_p denote the extended STM. Finally, we normalize STM_p. Let NSTM_p be a normalized version of STM_p as follows: $NSTM_p(F_1, F_2) = STM_p(F_1, F_2)/max(|F_1|, |F_2|)$ where $|F|$ denotes the number of nodes in F.

4.4 Flexibility of Metrics

Making assumptions on evaluation for a particular task and defining desiderata for a metric determine what evaluation scheme we are going to formulate. However, this kind of effort tends to make resulting evaluation metrics too restrictive to be reusable in other tasks. Such metrics might be adequate for that task, but we also value the flexibility of a metric that can be directly used or be easily extended to other tasks. To investigate the flexibility of MUC_p, BLANC_p and STM_p, we will examine these metrics without making the assumptions of twinless mentions and intransitivity of partial coreference against each metric. We consider that the assumption of link propagation is more fundamental and regard it as a basic premise, and thus we will continue to make that assumption.

MUC was originally designed to deal with response links spanning mentions that even key links do not reach. Thus, it is able to handle twinless mentions. If we do not assume intransitivity of partial coreference, we do not see any difficulty in changing the definition of correct links in MUC_p and making it capture transitive relations. Therefore, MUC_p does not require both assumptions of twinless mentions and intransitivity.

In contrast, BLANC was originally designed to handle true mentions in the gold standard. Since BLANC_p does not make any modifications on this aspect, it cannot deal with twinless mentions either. As for intransitivity, it is possible to easily change the definition of correct and incorrect links in BLANC_p to detect transitive relations. Thus, BLANC_p does not require intransitivity but does require the assumption of no twinless mentions.

Since STM_p simply matches elements in nodes as shown in Algorithm 1, it does not require the assumption of twinless mentions. With respect to intransitivity, we can extend STM_p by adding extra edges from a parent to grandchild nodes or others and applying Algorithm 1 to the modified trees. Hence, it does not require the assumption of intransitivity.

5 Experiments

To empirically examine the three metrics described in Section 4.2 and Section 4.3, we conducted an experiment using the artificial data shown in Table 1. Since BLANC_p cannot handle twinless mentions, we removed twinless mentions. We first created the gold standard shown in the first row of the table. It contains fifty events, twenty one singleton events, and seven event trees with three levels or less. We believe this distribution of partial coreference is representative of that of real data. We then created several system responses that are ordered toward two extremes. One extreme is all singletons in which they do not have correct links. The other is a single big tree that merges all event trees including singletons in the gold standard.

Figure 4 shows how the three metrics behave in two cases: (a) we increase the number of correct links from all singletons to the perfect output (equal to the gold standard), and (b) we increase the incorrect links from the perfect output to a single tree merging all trees in the gold standard. In the former case, we started with System 3 in Table 1. Next we added one correct link $28 \xrightarrow{s} 29$ shown in System 2. This way, we added correct links up to the perfect output one by one in a bottom-up fashion. In the latter case, we started

Response	Output
Gold standard	**(1(2(6))(3(7))(4)(5)) (8(9(11)(12))(10)) (13(14)(15)(16)(17)(18)) (19(20(21))(22)) (23(24)(25)) (26(27)) (28(29))** (30) (31) (32) (33) (34) (35) (36) (37) (38) (39) (40) (41) (42) (43) (44) (45) (46) (47) (48) (49) (50)
System 1	**(1(4)(5)(2(6))(3(7))) (8(9(11)(12))(10)) (13(18)(14)(15)(16)(17)) (19(22)(20(21))) (23(24)(25)) (26(27)) (28(29))** (30) (31) (32) (33) (34) (35) (36) (37) (38) (39) (40) (41) (42) (43) (44) (45) (46) (47) (48) **(49(50))**
System 2	(1) (2) (3) (4) (5) (6) (7) (8) (9) (10) (11) (12) (13) (14) (15) (16) (17) (18) (19) (20) (21) (22) (23) (24) (25) (26) (27) **(28(29))** (30) (31) (32) (33) (34) (35) (36) (37) (38) (39) (40) (41) (42) (43) (44) (45) (46) (47) (48) (49) (50)
System 3	(1) (2) (3) (4) (5) (6) (7) (8) (9) (10) (11) (12) (13) (14) (15) (16) (17) (18) (19) (20) (21) (22) (23) (24) (25) (26) (27) (28) (29) (30) (31) (32) (33) (34) (35) (36) (37) (38) (39) (40) (41) (42) (43) (44) (45) (46) (47) (48) (49) (50)

Table 1: Examples of a system response against a gold standard partial coreference. Each event tree is shown in the bold font and in the Newick standard format with parentheses.

with the perfect output, and then added one incorrect link $49 \xrightarrow{s} 50$ shown in System 1. In a manner similar to case (a), we added incorrect links up to the merged tree one by one in a bottom-up fashion.

The results indicate that MUC_p and BLANC_p meet the desiderata defined in Section 3.3 more adequately than NSTM_p. The curve of MUC_p and BLANC_p in Figure 4 are close to the linearity, which is practically useful as a metric. In contrast, NSTM_p fails to meet P4 and P5 in case (a), and fails to meet P5 in case (b). This is because STM first checks whether root nodes of two trees have the same element, and if the root nodes have different elements, STM stops searching the rest of nodes in the trees.

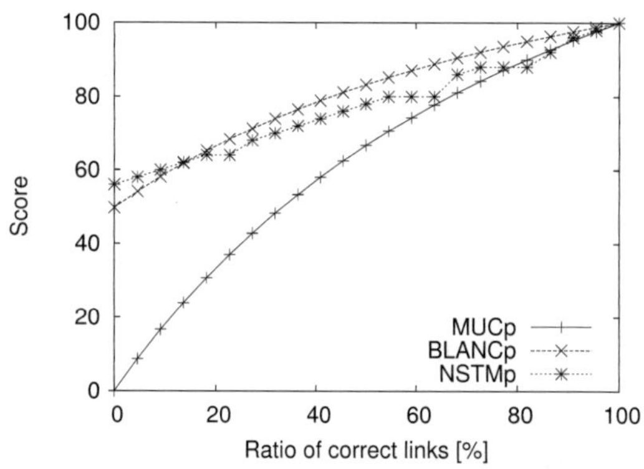

(a) The number of correct links increases from singletons to the perfect output (the gold standard) one by one.

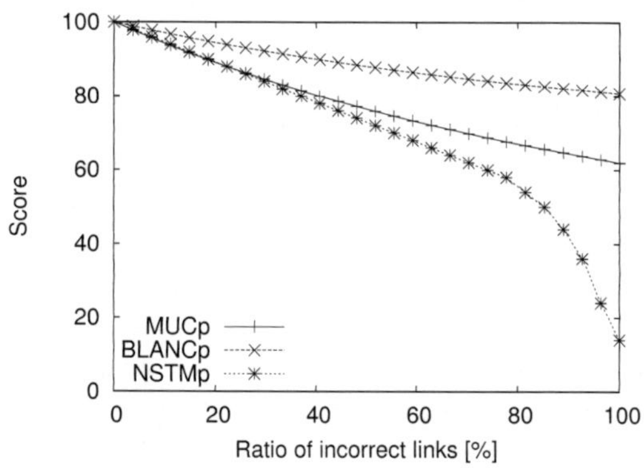

(b) The number of incorrect links increases from the perfect output to a single tree merging all trees one by one.

Figure 4: Score comparison among MUC_p, BLANC_p, and NSTM_p.

6 Discussion

In Section 4.4, we observed that MUC_p and STM_p are more flexible than BLANC_p because they can measure the performance coreference in the case of twinless mentions as well. The experimental results in Section 5 show that MUC_p and BLANC_p more adequate in terms of the five properties defined in Section 3.3. Putting these together, MUC_p seems the best metric for partial event coreference. However, MUC has two disadvantages that (1) it prefers systems that have more mentions per entity (event), and (2) it ignores recall for singletons (Pradhan et al., 2011). MUC_p also has these disadvantages. Thus, BLANC_p might be the best choice for partial coreference if we could assume that a system is given true mentions in the gold standard.

Although STM_p fails to satisfy P4 and P5, it has potential power to capture structural properties of partial coreference described in Section 3.3. This is because STM's recursive fashion of node-counting can be easily extend to counting the number of correct sibling relations.

7 Conclusion

We proposed an evaluation scheme for partial event coreference with conceptual event hierarchy constructed from mention-based event trees. We discussed possible assumptions that one can make, and examined extensions to three existing metrics. Our experimental results indicate that the extensions to MUC and BLANC are more adequate than the extension to STM. To our knowledge, this is the first work to argue an evaluation scheme for partial event coreference. Nevertheless, we believe that our scheme is generic and flexible enough to be applicable to other directed relations of events (e.g., causality and entailment) or other related tasks to compare hierarchical data based on unordered trees (e.g., ontology comparison). One future work is to improve the metrics by incorporating structural consistency of event trees as an additional property and implementing the metrics from the perspective of broad contexts beyond local evaluation by link-based counting.

8 Acknowledgements

This research was supported in part by DARPA grant FA8750-12-2-0342 funded under the DEFT program. Any opinions, findings, and conclusion or recommendations expressed in this material are those of the authors and do not necessarily reflect the view of the DARPA or the US government. We would like to thank anonymous reviewers for their helpful comments.

References

Amit Bagga and Breck Baldwin. 1998. Algorithms for Scoring Coreference Chains. In *Proceedings of LREC 1998 Workshop on Linguistics Coreference*, pages 563–566.

Cosmin Bejan and Sanda Harabagiu. 2010. Unsupervised Event Coreference Resolution with Rich Linguistic Features. In *Proceedings of ACL 2010*, pages 1412–1422.

Eric Bengtson and Dan Roth. 2008. Understanding the Value of Features for Coreference Resolution. In *Proceedings of EMNLP 2008*, pages 294–303.

Philip Bille. 2005. A Survey on Tree Edit Distance and Related Problems. *Theoretical Computer Science*, 337(1-3):217–239.

Jie Cai and Michael Strube. 2010. Evaluation Metrics For End-to-End Coreference Resolution Systems. In *Proceedings of SIGDIAL 2010*, pages 28–36.

Nathanael Chambers and Dan Jurafsky. 2008. Unsupervised Learning of Narrative Event Chains. In *Proceedings of ACL-HLT 2008*, pages 789–797.

Michael Collins and Nigel Duffy. 2001. Convolution Kernels for Natural Language. In *Proceedings of NIPS 2001*, pages 625–632.

Danilo Croce, Alessandro Moschitti, and Roberto Basili. 2011. Structured Lexical Similarity via Convolution Kernels on Dependency Trees. In *Proceedings of EMNLP 2011*, pages 1034–1046.

Erik D. Demaine, Shay Mozes, Benjamin Rossman, and Oren Weimann. 2009. An Optimal Decomposition Algorithm for Tree Edit Distance. *ACM Transactions on Algorithms (TALG)*, 6(1):2:1–2:19.

Greg Durrett, David Hall, and Dan Klein. 2013. Decentralized Entity-Level Modeling for Coreference Resolution. In *Proceedings of ACL 2013*, pages 114–124.

Michael Heilman and Noah A. Smith. 2010. Tree Edit Models for Recognizing Textual Entailments, Paraphrases, and Answers to Questions. In *Proceedings of NAACL-HLT 2013*, pages 1011–1019.

Eduard Hovy, Teruko Mitamura, Felisa Verdejo, Jun Araki, and Andrew Philpot. 2013. Events are Not Simple: Identity, Non-Identity, and Quasi-Identity. In *Proceedings of NAACL-HLT 2013 Workshop on Events: Definition, Detection, Coreference, and Representation*, pages 21–28.

Heng Ji, David Westbrook, and Ralph Grishman. 2005. Using Semantic Relations to Refine Coreference Decisions. In *Proceedings of EMNLP/HLT 2005*, pages 17–24.

Philip N. Klein. 1998. Computing the Edit-Distance Between Unrooted Ordered Trees. In *Proceedings of the 6th European Symposium on Algorithms (ESA)*, pages 91–102.

Emmanuel Lassalle and Pascal Denis. 2013. Improving pairwise coreference models through feature space hierarchy learning. In *Proceedings of ACL 2013*, pages 497–506.

Heeyoung Lee, Marta Recasens, Angel Chang, Mihai Surdeanu, and Dan Jurafsky. 2012. Joint Entity and Event Coreference Resolution across Documents. In *Proceedings of the Conference on Empirical Methods in Natural Language Processing and Computational Natural Language Learning (EMNLP-CoNLL)*, pages 489–500.

Xiaoqiang Luo. 2005. On Coreference Resolution Performance Metrics. In *Proceedings of EMNLP 2005*, pages 25–32.

Yashar Mehdad. 2009. Automatic Cost Estimation for Tree Edit Distance Using Particle Swarm Optimization. In *Proceedings of ACL-IJCNLP 2009*, pages 289–292.

Alessandro Moschitti, Daniele Pighin, and Roberto Basili. 2008. Tree Kernels for Semantic Role Labeling. *Computational Linguistics*, 34(2):193–224.

Mateusz Pawlik and Nikolaus Augsten. 2011. RTED: A Robust Algorithm for the Tree Edit Distance. *Proceedings of the VLDB Endowment (PVLDB)*, 5(4):334–345.

Sameer Pradhan, Lance Ramshaw, Mitchell Marcus, Martha Palmer, Ralph Weischedel, and Nianwen Xue. 2011. CoNLL-2011 Shared Task: Modeling Unrestricted Coreference in OntoNotes. In *Proceedings of CoNLL Shared Task 2011*, pages 1–27.

Altaf Rahman and Vincent Ng. 2009. Supervised Models for Coreference Resolution. In *Proceedings of EMNLP 2009*, pages 968–977.

Marta Recasens and Eduard Hovy. 2011. BLANC: Implementing the Rand index for coreference evaluation. *Natural Language Engineering*, 17(4):485–510.

Roger C. Schank and Robert P. Abelson. 1977. *Scripts, Plans, Goals, and Understanding: An Inquiry into Human Knowledge Structures*. Lawrence Erlbaum Associates.

Shashank Srivastava, Dirk Hovy, and Eduard Hovy. 2013. A Walk-Based Semantically Enriched Tree Kernel Over Distributed Word Representations. In *Proceedings of EMNLP 2013*, pages 1411–1416.

Veselin Stoyanov, Nathan Gilbert, Claire Cardie, and Ellen Riloff. 2009. Conundrums in Noun Phrase Coreference Resolution: Making Sense of the State-of-the-Art. In *Proceedings of ACL/IJCNLP 2009*, pages 656–664.

Kuo-Chung Tai. 1979. The Tree-to-Tree Correction Problem. *Journal of the ACM (JACM)*, 26(3):422–433.

Marc Vilain, John Burger, John Aberdeen, Dennis Connolly, and Lynette Hirschman. 1995. A Model-Theoretic Coreference Scoring Scheme. In *Proceedings of the 6th Message Understanding Conference (MUC)*, pages 45–52.

Mengqiu Wang and Christopher D. Manning. 2010. Probabilistic Tree-Edit Models with Structured Latent Variables for Textual Entailment and Question Answering. In *Proceedings of COLING 2010*, pages 1164–1172.

Wuu Yang. 1991. Identifying Syntactic Differences Between Two Programs. *Software: Practice and Experience*, 21(7):739–755.

Xuchen Yao, Benjamin Van Durme, Chris Callison-burch, and Peter Clark. 2013. Answer Extraction as Sequence Tagging with Tree Edit Distance. In *Proceedings of NAACL-HLT 2013*, pages 858–867.

Kaizhong Zhang and Dennis Shasha. 1989. Simple Fast Algorithms for the Editing Distance Between Trees and Related Problems. *SIAM J. Comput.*, 18(6):1245–1262.

Author Index